ARISE
JERUSALEM!

Gary Manley

OMEGA
HOUSE
PUBLISHING

Three Rivers, Michigan

Published by Omega House Publishing
P.O. Box 68
Three Rivers, Michigan 49093-9068

Cover design by Mazzocchi Group 616-273-7070

ISBN 0-9672519-1-5

Library of Congress Catalog Card Number:

Printed in the United States of America.

ARISE
JERUSALEM!

CONTENTS

ACKNOWLEDGMENTS   7
PREFACE   9

CHAPTER 1 —AN ENSIGN TO THE NATIONS   13
CHAPTER 2 —IN SUCH A TIME AS THIS   21
   Discerning Times and Seasons
   Generation of Change
CHAPTER 3 —PLANET EARTH UNDER RESTORATION   29
   God's Working Today in the Land
   A Remembrance of eternal Love and Unity
   God's Peace Through Obedience
   Peace in the Future
   Guidelines for True Peace
   Prophetic Anointing
   A Physical Kingdom
   Authority
CHAPTER 4 —GOD'S PROPHETIC TIME CLOCK   49
   Prophetic Signs
   The False Dove
   Shophar
   Additional Prophetic Signs
   Emerging Markets
CHAPTER 5 —GOD'S INHERITANCE   61
   Specific Instructions Regarding Prophecy
   Prophesy Against Evil Leadership
   Prophesy Against Rebellious Nations
   Prophesy Blessings to Israel
   Prophesy to the People
   The Land Called Judah
   The Place Called Jerusalem
   A Veiled Jewel
   A City Named by God
   Jerusalem and the Great Holy Spirit Fires

CHAPTER 6 —A ROSE BLOOMS   85
    The Nation of Israel in the World
    Time to Listen to the God of Israel
CHAPTER 7 —A WINDOW OF OPPORTUNITY   103
    Visitors
    An Opportunity
    Blessed to be a Blessing
    Doing God's Pleasure a Second Time
CHAPTER 8 —GOD'S REVELATION REQUIRES A RESPONSE 115
    Cyrus Anointed by God
    Shepherd
    Perform All My Pleasure
    Proclaming the Restoration of Jerusalem
    Foundation of the Temple
    Anointed
    The Responsibility of Wealth
    The Kingdom View
    A Scriptural Model for Mercy and Blessings
    Five Fold Prophecy
    Fulfilling God's Pleasure
    Response of the Gentile Church
    Calling Forth, Arise Jerusalem
CHAPTER 9 —GOD REQUIRES MERCY   137
    A Practical Application and Response
    Manifestations of Mercy
    Mercy: A Requirement
    Mercy Defined
    Genuine Mercy
    Bible Instruction on Mercy
    Power of Mercy
    Promises of Mercy
    Being Filled with Mercy
CHAPTER 10 —DOING GOD'S PLEASURE   143
CHAPTER 11 —CONCLUSION   151

PROSE AND PROPHECIES

Arise, Jerusalem 14
A Time and A Season 19
Waiting 25
On the Edge 28
Time for Heavenly Peace 39
Master Engraver 43
Today's Mountains, Tomorrow's Plains 45
Full Anointing on the Land 57
The Whirlwind 62
The Oppressors 64
The Friends of God 65
Nations of Oppression 66
Prophesy Jubilee to the Holy Land 67
Men of Wisdom 68
Now is the Time to Speak 69
Hills of Praise 71
End of Mourning in Judea 72
The Holy City 77
The Great Controversy 78
Holy Spirit Blow A Gentle Breath Over the Land 81
Glory of the Ages 82
A City with Eternal Blessings 100
Arise, Queen of Cities 111
Jerusalem Restored 120
Rejoicing and Praise 131
A New Day 135
A Garden of Eden 154

Acknowledgments

First of all, I want to thank my friend the Holy Spirit for the words of this book; arranging it to work for the glory of the Lord God of Israel.

I would like to thank my publisher and all those who had input in the physical making of this book. And especially, the encouragement from my wife and friend Zendra to complete *Arise Jerusalem!*

This book was written in Israel during various trips. The prose was given to me by the Holy Spirit as I prayed in the wilderness regions of Israel.

PREFACE

Arise Jerusalem is a call, yet even a warning, to both individuals and nations to become concerned about and bless Israel and the Holy Land. Arise Jerusalem is a call to those who love God to bless His nation and people. Arise Jerusalem is a call to those who do not love God's people, to repent and seek God's face. Arise Jerusalem is a prophetic letter to Israel and Jerusalem to arise into God's glory. Throughout the book prophetic messages call forth the land and people.

According to Haggai chapter one, blessing Israel is not an option for those who want God's blessings. Scriptures clearly present Israel and Jerusalem as God's desire and His love. Additional Scriptures teach that ones relationship with God is influenced by ones actions and attitudes toward the nation of Israel and the Jewish people, Ezekiel chapters 24-29. We bless God when we take an interest in his desires and love the things that He loves. Further we are told to pray for and bless Jerusalem (Ps 122). Also, blessings and comfort are given to those who bless Israel (Ps 122 and Isa 66) and Jerusalem.

The church in North America (as well as other regions) is making a serious mistake by consuming great wealth on its carnal delights and not being concerned for Israel (read Amos) and the things of God. If the wealthy churches in America and other rich nations do not repent of their selfish consumption, destruction will be sure to come. It is time to hear the Holy Spirit and stop listening to the words of men determined to promote their own ways and interest out of greed.

This book makes no attempt to discuss eschatology or give any bias toward any particular view point. Many different theories exist regarding end time events and many books have been published on the subject. Yet, they are largely conjecture because the Holy Spirit has not revealed many truths regarding this subject.

Regardless of ones personal view on such things, the fact remains that the Bible clearly instructs the believers in Jesus Christ to bless Jerusalem and Israel, including the land, the nation, and the people. That scriptural instruction has little to do with our particular view on eschatology. As believers we are responsible to obey God's instruction each day and act on that which is revealed. Our actions today are not made based on some event or projected events that will happen at some future time, but obedience each day as the Holy Spirit directs our steps. Faith always operates in the present. Clearly, God is regathering and rebuilding Israel and Jerusalem at this time. God requires our response in the present, not in the future. Believers are to proclaim the Gospel of Christ, not second guess God's activities.

If we have any sign or basis on which to project future events it centers on the nation of Israel and specifically on Jerusalem (Isa 18:3). Old Testament prophecies speak at great length regarding Israel's final restoration and the nations pivotal role in God's plan to establish His kingdom on this earth.

Israel is specifically spoken of as a sign to the nations in both Isaiah chapter 11 and Haggai. In Matthew chapter 24, Jesus also reminds us to watch Israel. Israel and Jerusalem are the parameters which God has given us to understand end time events. Israel is the instrument that God is using and will use to bring glory to His mighty name.

The nation of Israel is a great end time prophetic clock. The nation is a baseline to evaluate and understand events on the earth and how they relate to God's eternal plan. All world events of prophetic importance must now be evaluated in relationship to Israel.

Jerusalem and the nation of Israel continue to send forth an endless flow of prophetic pieces that fit into God's great puzzle of heavenly and earthly events as the two aspects of God's kingdoms merge under Jesus. God's clock continues to move ahead each day towards the establishment of His earthly "kingdom of heaven." Israel continues to be (specifically Jerusalem) God's sign and source of revelation to the nations of the earth regarding His workings.

What God does is always through His Holy Spirit, not through the ways of man. It is exciting to live in a time when God's Holy Spirit is actively working in Israel to accomplish His perfect plan. God used an Old Testament nation (Israel) to establish His "Kingdom of Heaven" through Jesus Christ. In a like manner as

Jesus prepares Jerusalem for His throne, He is preparing an earthly kingdom that will foreshadow future events. Present day Israel is the establishment of this earthly phase of His working. Prior to the establishment of the "New Jerusalem" God will establish the city of Jerusalem as a world headquarters. We currently see the "Kingdom of David" being newly established in Jerusalem. Believers are called to be partners in this process.

God may very well allow the destruction of much of what is being built today in the Holy Land in the years ahead before He establishes His throne in Jerusalem. Still, what God is doing in the Holy Land today is a fulfillment of prophecy and a sign to all nations of the earth. The church is called to be a partner with God.

The New Testament church has been grafted into the true vine, yet the root and vine remain always the same. As God grafts Israel back into the true vine, Israel and the church will become one as they receive from the same root and vine. No one has replaced anyone! In Christ there is no Jew or Greek, no male or female. In Christ all who believe are one and all Israel will believe (Ro 11:20). Look at God's creation. Nature shows us that in order to graft a new or additional branch onto the vine, nothing has to be removed. Also grafts can be added and removed by the gardener at his will. The vine will support more than one branch at a time! Can not all who believe be branches of the same vine and receive of the same nutrients and therefore produce the same kind of fruit (John chapter 15)? Those who come to God must come by faith in Jesus. There is no other way (Heb 11:6).

Chapter 1

An Ensign To The Nations

"And he shall set up an ensign for the nations, and shall assemble the outcasts of Israel, and gather together the dispersed of Judah from the four corners of the earth."

—*Isaiah 11:12*

What is this land called Israel? Why do the Kings of the earth rant and rave over this little city called Jerusalem? Why do the nations of the earth tremble at events in a tiny portion of land called the Holy Land? So much fighting over this tiny section of land when the earth is so big.

Then the Lord reminded me, "it is my place— my special land. Israel is my portion of the earth, I'm married to that land and my Son's blood rests in that land."

"Open your spiritual eyes and look and see in the spiritual realm. The conflict is a spiritual warfare. Be not deceived by what you hear and see around you, but look up and be shown by the Holy Spirit who receives truth directly from the Father."

"It is from my Holy City that I will manifest my glory to the whole earth. It is from my Holy City that I will destroy all the powers of darkness. All the power in the universe is at hand to accomplish every one of my promises regarding Jerusalem and the Holy Land. Not a single word I have spoken will be forgotten. For in my anger over the controversy for my chosen city the nations of the earth will be destroyed (Isaiah 33). I have promised to end this controversy in a single day. Then the name of the Lord God of Israel will be glorified and my land and people can rest."

Then the Lord said, "sing new songs to my land, songs for a new season that I will take delight in for my glory. Songs of vision, songs of prophecy, songs of hope, and songs to call forth a new thing that I desire. For now is the time, the vision is fulfilled."

"Cry yet, saying, Thus saith the Lord of hosts; My cities through prosperity shall yet be spread abroad; and the Lord shall yet comfort Zion, and shall yet choose Jerusalem."

—Zechariah 1:17

Arise, Jerusalem

Arise, Jerusalem and Israel.
Adorn yourself with your royal apparel.
Prepare for your King, Jerusalem.

Make straight His way from the East.
Let His cherubim of glory alight upon thee.
Your name shall arise above every mountain.

You are an ensign for the nations.
Let them observe your wonders, Jerusalem.
The appointed time has come, Israel.

Be filled with the glory of Kings.
Let the sea and the land bless you from afar.
Make ready the harvest festival.

You are a chosen land and people.
Let your blessings flow to you, Jerusalem.
Shine as the sun forever, Israel.

Arise to your high place, Holy City.
Let your King be seated in your midst.
Honor is yours forever and ever.

Jerusalem, Jerusalem, Jerusalem.
Let dancing and joy fill your streets.
Jerusalem, Israel be filled.

Is today "that day" the prophet Isaiah was talking about so many years ago? Today again for the second time we see the remnant of God's people being recovered from all regions of the earth to fill the land of promise (Isa 11:11).

Along with the regathering process the nation of Israel and Jerusalem are being built. Israel and Judah are united as one people in peace, Isaiah 11:12 says these events are an ensign for the nations of the earth. Is it the same "that day" for which Zerubbabel was made a signet (Hag 2:23)?

It is essential to understand that Israel is God's witness (Isa 43:10) and a sign (Isa 11:12) to the nations of the earth. In many respects present day Israel is the heartbeat of the earth. God speaks to the whole earth through events in Israel. In fact, if we miss what God is doing and saying through Israel, we will miss important aspects of what God is revealing to us. The nation of Israel is like an endless prophetic river that has great significance for our times regarding both heaven and earth.

In addition to prophetic significance, Israel and the Holy Land also have great practical influence on our daily lives. What God is doing in Israel affects almost every aspect of our daily lives, and this influence will continue to increase as God reorders the world system around His ways. Examples that affect our daily lives include the following:

1. Conflict with Arab nations affects oil prices, which in turn affect world economies.
2. Jews leaving nations affect national governments.
3. Relationships with Israel affect cooperation and military alliances between nations.

4. National relationships with Israel also determine how God
   views nations and whether they receive blessings or curses
   from heaven. This affects many aspects of peoples daily lives.
5. The battle over Jerusalem is setting the stage and national
   alignments for the next world war.

Could it be that the Lord of Hosts is telling His church and the
nations of the earth it is now time for the holy vision to be con-
summated? Is now that time when His Spirit is moving over the
land to accomplish God's final plans regarding Jerusalem and the
second coming of Messiah Jesus?

I believe the Lord is declaring the time is well advanced, even
now the time is at hand. Today (now) is the opportunity to make
straight the way in the Holy Land for the return of Messiah Jesus!

Yet, today people say, as in the era of Haggai, "the time is not
come" (Hag 1:2). People continue to live in their ceiled houses
while the House of God and Holy Land lie in need. Would God say
to this generation today, "Consider your ways" (Hag 1). Is today
the time to go gather supplies and build the Lord's place that He
will take pleasure and be glorified (Hag 1:7)?

Until the church obeys and fears before the Lord, spiritual and
national drought will prevail, and the dew of heaven will be stayed
as in the time of the prophet Haggai (Hag 1:9-11).

*"Ye looked for much, and, lo, it came to little; and when ye brought it
home, I did blow upon it. Why? saith the Lord of hosts. Because of mine
house that is waste, and ye run every man unto his own house. Therefore,
the heaven over you is stayed from dew, and the earth is stayed from her
fruit."*

The body of Christ must take a new look at its priorities; building fancy church structures and large organizations may not be the
primary focus of God's desires. Jesus and the early church did not
attach much importance to such activities. The world's ways is to
build material wealth, but the church is to build spiritual wealth.
The world accumulates material things, the church distributes
things of the kingdom. Obedience to God's ways always brings
spiritual life and blessings, but attention to man's ways always
brings judgements and spiritual death. Only by obedience can the

true life and blessings of God be obtained. As we see in the book of Haggai, two results will follow obedience. One, obedience to building the Land of Israel will cause the Spirit of God to go forth and stir up the spirit of the people (Hag 1:14). Two, the blessings of the Lord will follow once the foundation is started, even from the day it was started and upward (Hag 2:18)!

Now is the time for gentiles to be about the work described in Isaiah 60:8-11: To bring the people of Zion with blessings to the land of Israel, to build up the walls and minister unto the Holy City and its people God's mercy. Day and night the favor of the nations of the world must flow into Jerusalem (Isa 60:8-11).

This is God's will and purpose for the land that His name be glorified. As a result, all of God's people who hear and obey will rejoice with Jerusalem and be comforted within her walls (Isa 66:10-14).

Is not the Lord's working in Israel an ensign to the nations as to the time in which we live and to His church an ensign to be partners in making straight the way? Is not the ministry of Zerubbabel a signet, a seal to the indubitable plan of God regarding the completion of His pleasure? Are not the proclamation and accomplishments of Cyrus instructions regarding "that day", yet is today "that day"?

Just as John the Baptist prepared the way for the first coming of Jesus, even while Jesus walked the earth prior to His public ministry. Now the church must prepare the way for the second coming of Jesus, even while the Holy Land is springing forth with the new thing and being filled with God's remnant to wait their coming Messiah. The work and preparation are going forth according to God's schedule. The only question that remains is who will hear and get involved in God's program?

For if today is "that day," it is time, (yes, it is even urgent) to get busy and prepare the way for the King of Kings and Lord of Lords. Gentile believers must understand they are obligate partners in preparing the way for Jesus to return to Jerusalem.

Jerusalem is the city where everything involving God's plan for the earth is centered. Throughout history the most extraordinary events involving God, angels, and men have occurred in the Holy Land, Many prophecies yet to be fulfilled will also involve additional events in the Holy Land. Yet, even now these kinds of extraordinary events involving God's heavenly messengers are occurring in Jerusalem.

Jerusalem even now is starting to see her destiny fulfilled as God again declares Jerusalem His holy habitation on earth and prepares for Jerusalem's temple to be His holy oblation.

As Jesus prepares to return to Jerusalem with His heavenly host, His land and people must be prepared as a foreshadowing of the coming glorious kingdom. Following the completion of this earthly phase God will unite His heavenly and earthly kingdoms as the New Jerusalem appears on earth with all of its glory.

Prior to that event the promises made to King David must be fulfilled. Events taking place in the Holy Land and particularly Jerusalem currently point to the establishment and soon return of David's Kingdom in preparation for Christ's return to earth. This is a part of God's call to all the inhabitants of the earth to see God's workings and signs on the earth. *"All ye inhabitants of the world, and dwellers on the earth, see ye, when he lifteth up an ensign on the mountains; and when he bloweth a trumpet, hear ye"* (Isa 18:3). The manifestations are set forth for all to see, God's earthly kingdom in Jerusalem must reflect the glory of King David and finally the full glory of King Jesus.

Now is the time to look, see and become involved. What a tragedy to have lived in a time of great manifestations from heaven and yet to have missed one of the greatest events of all times because of complacency, or to have been blinded by the traditions of men's ways. Would the established church of today repeat the mistake of the Jewish leaders in Jesus' time who missed their Messiah due to their religious traditions and hardness of heart?

A Time and A Season

Now is the time and season to call forth.
Arise, Jerusalem and Israel.

Awaken to your eternal destiny, great city.
Your hour has come, glorious land.
The Lord of Lords and King of Kings is coming.

His throne is in the midst of your sanctuary.
Be filled with joy and everlasting songs.
Arise and look toward the East for glory comes.

Rivers of life shall flow from the midst of you.
The dry land and the sea around you shall find new life.
Abundance shall flow from your sanctuary.

The time of harvest has come, Jerusalem.
The sweet fruit rests heavy on the vine, most holy city.
Awaken and arise, Jerusalem and Israel.

Chapter 2

In Such A Time As This

*"Again the second time the Lord shall regather his
people from the four corners of the earth,"*
—Isa 11:11
*"even saying to Jerusalem, thou shalt be built;
and to the temple. Thy foundation shall be laid."*
—Isa 44:28

Toward the end of an age about two thousand years ago, the nation of Israel had yet one great function to complete in God's plan for the earth while they remained in the promised land. The nation of Israel was set apart to bring forth Jesus Christ and through Him the gift of salvation to all peoples. Following the earthly ministry of Jesus and the Holy Spirit outpouring on the early church, the nation of Israel disappeared among the nations of the world as a gentile church emerged under the leadership of the Holy Spirit. The gentile nations through Jesus had been commissioned with the gospel and the new church that would take the gospel to all the nations of the earth began to be anointed by the Holy Spirit.

Today we are approaching the end of that gentile age as God's time table of events moves ahead. However, I believe as we approach the end of this phase of God's plan the gentile church has yet one great purpose to fulfill. Perhaps this will take place even as the gentile church passes out of the spot light, and the new, combined Jewish-Gentile church that will receive Christ emerges in Jerusalem.

In God's plan, Israel gave the gentile people the gift of Christ and salvation. In like manner the gentile believers must now return this mercy and be instrumental in opening the door for the nation of Israel to receive salvation and the mercy of God (Ro 11). The faithful segment within the Church of Jesus Christ among the gentile nations has yet to complete its part in building Jerusalem and laying the foundation for the temple. Gentile believers must continue to be partners in preparing the way for Jesus in Jerusalem and the Holy Land.

This may be one of the final undertakings for the gentile believers during this church age. What a glorious opportunity to do the pleasure of God even as the gentile nations and the apostate religious systems of this world sink deeper and deeper into deception.

Yet, we live in an exciting and dynamic time. A time like no other in history. A time that many have wanted to experience but only saw as a shadow of things to come. A season of time that God's prophets throughout the ages have talked about and that all creation waits for with anticipation. A season of time that even the angels in heaven watch with amazement.

Today, those who look up toward heaven will be shown these glorious times and be filled with the joy and excitement of the season. Yet, those who look around them and are captivated by earthly concerns will find despair, hopelessness and impending disaster on every side. For those with an earthly vision this will be a time of great confusion and turmoil.

As the Holy Spirit moves the glory of the church to Jerusalem in preparation for the return of Jesus, the believers in America (and other gentile nations) have yet this window of opportunity to help prepare the way of the Lord by helping to prepare Jerusalem to receive her King.

Those who love God will love what God loves and seek to be a part of fulfilling His plan in the holy land. Today is truly a time of opportunity like no other generation has ever experienced. However, opportunities have to be seized at the appropriate time before they are lost forever.

Discerning Times and Seasons

The changing of the seasons is a common occurrence on earth. Change brings fulfillment of that which is complete and the hope of newness of that which will be fulfilled. The changing of the seasons frequently manifest signs of change as an indication of what is taking place and an indication of what to expect in the future, such as the coloring of the leaves in the Fall or the first green grass of Spring, or the shifting winds ahead of a storm. God also gives us signs in the spiritual realm to remind us of His promises, which helps us understand what He is doing and encourages us with expectations for the future.

In Matthew chapter 16, Jesus talks about being able to discern natural events, but being unable to discern spiritual events. God's people are expected to discern spiritual times and be a part of what God is doing. Yet, it is clear in Scriptures that throughout history the majority of religious people were unable to discern the times spiritually and as a result they have missed what God was doing in their time of opportunity, often due to long held traditions of men which made the things of God to no effect in their lives (Mk 7:13).

It appears that this world is currently experiencing some momentous signs of the end times. For example on the world front: rising of the many new nations and regions to economic power (often called emerging markets), worldwide prosperity; developments in China; changes in European nations, changes to the North to Russia, the Balkan wars, problems in Southern Russia such as Chechnyu and Tajikistan and expansion of NATO along the lines of conflict. Examples in the Mideast region include: countries like Syria and Iran increasing their military power; the obsession of some mid-east nations to harm Israel and any other nation or nations that are friends with or support Israel; relationships between Russia, Iran and other mideast nations; many of the old enemies of Israel demonstrating open hostility; a strong spirit of anti-christ moving from this region throughout the earth, particularly into the free world nations of Europe and North America. Examples in Israel include the enhanced development of the Jewish nation; Jewish people coming home from all parts of the world in large numbers; a cry for peace across the Holy Land by both sides; a spiritual awakening in Israel (currently taking many forms). There are growing numbers of believers being called to Jerusalem from all parts of the earth, both Jews and gentiles; an increasing remnant of Jewish believers. We also see signs in the church such as a growing Christian Arab church in regions of the Mid-east, and at the same time a falling away of the Christian church in most nations of the free world, including the destruction and apostate activities of numerous gentile churches and ministries.

Current signs are forecasting world changing events to come shortly. Yet most of the church establishment is unconcerned and preoccupied with trivial activities and how daily events will affect their personal enjoyment. The God of mammon has blinded the hearts and minds of most church people. End time wealth and world prosperity is a deception that the religious world has grasped with both hands. Many churches have entered a complacent dormancy and are enjoying a comatose utopian experience. Like the blind leading the blind they are deceiving and being deceived. As the Pharisees of Jesus' day, too many modern Christians are able to discern natural events and how they affect their natural lives, but are unable to discern the spiritual realm and heavenly events (Mt 16:1-5). Unfortunately, many of these people will awaken too late and be unprepared like the five foolish virgins (Mt 25:1-13). The Christian religious system has been deceived by money and building ministries rather than being obedient to the commands of Jesus.

The signs of God's event time table are telling us today that one of the greatest events in the history of this earth is unfolding before us with great speed. The fulfillment of everything we know is about to be completed. As a result the whole earth is going to change completely. We live on the threshold of change so dramatic that events will shake the very foundations of civilization across the earth. Yet, these events will come quickly, seemingly without warning. Only those to whom the Holy Spirit reveals these events will have understanding. Those without spiritual discernment will be swept away by this great river of divine events to a sea of destruction. To those who can hear, awaken and prepare now! Jesus said, *"the flesh profiteth nothing: the words that I speak unto you, they are spirit, and they are life"* (Jn 6:63). God is speaking clearly in these days, yet few can hear! We live in the days like the days of Noah. Many are watching, talking and some are even working on the ark, but only a remnant will enter into the kingdom of God before the doors are closed.

Waiting

The bridegroom hath prepared for the feast day.
The bride waits with patient expectation.
The sanctuary is filled with lamps of oil.

The hour is late, turmoil and darkness fill the streets.
Yet, the bride waits in peaceful expectation for the call.
A voice, from the bridegroom.

The quiet lamps sit beside the resting bride.
Flask filled with pure olive oil rest in place.
Expectant ears listen for the impending call.

The unseen partner on the wall ticks off each second.
Will the next tick bring the long awaited call.
All is ready, all is set in place, Jerusalem waits.

Jesus forecasted dramatic changes during His time on earth (Mt 24). Following the return of Jesus to heaven, the Holy Spirit led the early church regarding these impending changes (Ac 4:32-37). The Holy Spirit knew that all the material things believers had accumulated would all be gone in a few years. As a result, the early believers were led to use these things to bless others. Are we living in a similar time?

Perhaps all the things that we enjoy and take for granted will be gone in a few years. Should the church today be using more of its wealth to help others instead of building self-indulgent icons which will be destroyed during the season of change?

The "generation of change" in which we live is in many ways analogous to the "generation of change" in which Jesus lived and in which the Bible was written. Jesus and the believers in the early church recorded in Acts were God's messengers during the end of an age. Simultaneously, during this time, God was establishing the "new thing" even as the new church was springing forth and the New Testament was being written.

Today, we are in the final years of that gentile church age and the "new thing" of God is taking life in Israel with great power. Today, as in the time of Jesus, the "old thing" is on the edge of death, while nothing is able to hold back the "new thing" that God is doing. Again in our time, simultaneously, the time of the fulfillment of the vision is upon us as the "new thing" receives life from the Lord God of Israel to complete His plan (Isa 43:19). Those that hold on to the "old thing" (the religious traditions) will experience the same fate as the Jewish religious leaders that refused to accept Jesus as their Messiah.

Generation of Change
(Mt 24:32-33; Lk 21:24; Ro 11:20, 25; 2 Th 2:3)

In Jesus' time, Israel was a defined nation. Jesus walked the earth as a part of that nation, its people and religious system. He called the nation to repent and believe at the edge of destruction. Jesus was born into an evil generation, in both political and religious aspects: a tarnished pearl that was beyond hope and about to be hidden among the nations (Mt 13:44).

As the gentile church emerged, God poured out His favor upon a spiritual nation hidden among the gentile nations of the earth (Mt 13:45-46). This people and their nations were given the responsibility of proclaiming the gospel of Jesus Christ to the world as believers became the temple of God through the infilling of the Holy Spirit.

Therefore, today it is important to understand that Israel is again a defined nation in the promised land waiting for the fulfillment of the promise. This initiates a new "generation of change." Israel today, sits in the midst of a dark desert as a great bright light on a high hill, as a sign to all nations and peoples regarding the time and season of this day. The very presence of Israel in current form speaks of the impending powerful hand of God prepared to move over the earth in fulfillment of many long standing prophecies and bring glory to his name across the earth and heavens. Israel is also a prophetic sign that reveals impending doom on all that represents sin and unrighteousness as God stands prepared to enter with the armies of a righteous kingdom to claim what is His.

On the Edge

All through the heavenly host is stillness.
Crowns are laid at the Master's feet.
Expectation is moving across the heavens.

The trumpet is at the angel's mouth,
on the edge of the throne.
The heavenly messengers look and wait for the command.
The armies of God are positioned on the edge of heaven.

The earth is in confusion as a restless sea.
Men run to and fro across the whole earth,
crying peace, peace.
The expectation and stillness of heaven is missed.

The bride cries out, "O Lord Jesus come!"
The Holy Spirit has stirred the hearts of God's people.
The lamps and flasks of olive oil are held close at hand.

Glory hovers over Jerusalem as an anointing cloud.
The walls are being strengthened at the foundations.
Prosperity is starting to rain as a flood from heaven.

The watchmen stand on the East wall of the holy city.
Watching for glory to break forth towards Jerusalem.
Even as rays of light are starting to break in the East.

My spirit cries within me, even now.
Lord Jesus let the trumpet sound loud and clear.
Let heaven and earth be united under your glory.

Chapter 3

PLANET EARTH UNDER RESTORATION

"For behold, I create new heavens and a new earth: and
the former shall not be remembered, nor come to mind."
—Isaiah 65:17

What is happening on the earth today is not business as usual. We live during a unique time because God is in the initial stages of totally reordering and restoring everything associated with planet earth in preparation for Jesus to establish His heavenly kingdom in Jerusalem. As God restores planet earth back to its original created state of perfection everything must be purified and reordered so that every aspect of earth will again reflect the glory of God in its fullness. The earth and its inhabitants must be restored to unity with God's heavenly kingdom. As a result, all that is out of unity must be destroyed and or restored.

For those who are out of unity with God, this process will be a fearful time filled with great confusion and turmoil. This is because God will allow the sin process to exhaust itself throughout the earth (Romans chapter one gives the pattern for this process). If people want to follow Satan's ways over God's way, He will let them see what sin is really like. In reality, God is in perfect control of every situation to accomplish His perfect purpose in a very orderly and predictable manner.

However, man has no basis to understand what is taking place because he has no historical record to study. Only the Bible gives prophetic insights as to the time in which we live, the magnitude of what is taking place, and what the outcome will be.

One thing is clear in Scripture, that Israel will play a major role in the reordering process, and Israel is the key to understanding present day times and events. Jesus said in Matthew 6:22, *"The light (lamp) of the body is the eye."* In Deuteronomy 32:10, Israel is kept as the apple of God's eye. Israel is the center of God's focus, but it is also the light that reveals God to the nations of the earth (Isa 43:10-12)! Also, Israel will become the center of the reordered earth as God sets up His kingdom in Jerusalem (Isa 60:12-13).

The Spirit of the living God is already at work throughout the world preparing the way for this renovation of the earth and a renaissance of God's glory. The nation of Israel is the primary signal and witness to the nations of the earth regarding the workings of God on planet earth in these last days, read Matthew chapter 24 and Luke chapter 21. God is in this day speaking clearly to the nations and peoples of the earth through Israel regarding His plans and the times and season in which this generation lives.

I expect on God's map of the earth, Israel is the center of the world. As a result, Israel and the Holy Land are rapidly becoming the center of world attention as God continues to make straight His way in the land. Therefore, a clear perception of God's desire for Israel and the Holy Land holds the key to a clear understanding of world events on the earth today. World events are not random or isolated, everything conforms to a divine plan and purpose. *"They are the eyes of the Lord, which run to and fro through the whole earth"* (Zec 4:10). As a result of this divine authority over events on earth, an understanding of world events today requires a comprehension of the spiritual dimension. In reality, only the Holy Spirit can provide an accurate interpretation of world events, because only the Holy Spirit knows the mind of God. Subsequently, only those shown and led by the Holy Spirit can have a true understanding of current world events.

Since Israel became a nation we find that, increasingly, world events are held hostage to the spiritual warfare between God's heavenly kingdom and the kingdoms of this earth (under the influence of Satan). This is the result of Satan's attempts to sidetrack God's plan for Jerusalem. Many of the problems in the world today correlate to the spiritual battle for the control of Jerusalem. The malicious desire to control Jerusalem will be the demise of many nations in the years ahead. *"I am jealous for Jerusalem and for Zion with a great jealousy"* (Zec 1:14).

Yet, during this time, the call of God to each person remains the same as it has throughout the years. John the Baptist, Jesus, and the early church all proclaimed the same truth. The word of God to each person alive today is: repent and believe in Jesus Christ as the Son of the living God of Israel. What the world needs is a personal relationship with Jesus Christ!

Those who look to Jesus have nothing to fear. In fact, this change is a glorious thing for believers because it means being with Christ. It also means a restoration to unity with Christ for God's earth. All the earth waits for these glorious events!

God's Workings Today in the Land

What is God doing in Israel today? What is God restoring and preparing? The answer is that God is doing many things. Many of these things signal the indubitable soon return of Jesus. Some of these things are discussed below*.

*Bringing Together All Things

I believe one of the major things God is doing currently is bringing about the completion of the Scripture given in Ephesians 1:10, *"That in the dispensation of the fullness of times he might gather together in one all things in Christ, both which are in heaven, and which are on earth; even in him.*" Not only will He bring heaven and earth together, but in this process, Jesus will make peace on earth by bringing all men together (Jews and Gentiles) as one, *"For he is our peace, who had made both one, and hath broken down the middle wall of partition between us"* (Eph 2:14).

In the early part of Genesis is recorded the establishment of God's earthly kingdom. This kingdom was established as a part of His heavenly kingdom and the two were in perfect unity. We see this as God came and walked in His garden and talked with man as a friend, as in Genesis chapters 2 and 3. What God does always brings unity.

As a result of sin, the earthly kingdom lost unity with the heavenly. However, God in His great mercy established a way to restore unity through Jesus Christ. By divine wisdom, the nation of Israel became the channel for this process. Israel is to play a key role in establishing unity between heaven and earth.

A Remembrance of Love and Unity

When God established the nation of Israel, He initiated a divine order of worship and also created symbols of remembrance that men would not forget their Creator. As a part of the tabernacle and worship for the nation of Israel, one of these powerful symbols, is called the Menorah. Interestingly the Menorah was closely associated with the burning of incense, which was another aspect of national worship. Both are important for worship and as remembrances.

As a symbol, the Menorah is represented in both the heavenly and earthly realm of God's kingdom. One of the expressions portrayed by the Menorah is the eternal love relationship (marriage relationship) between God and His people as well as His creation. Secondly, the Menorah is a remembrance of the eternal unity between heaven and earth. God created both in perfect unity and will again restore that fullness of unity. The Menorah also represents the interdependence of each on the other. For example, Israel can do nothing without God and yet God has set Israel aside as the instrument to bring glory to His name. When associated with the olive tree (Zec 4:1-7) or with the olive branch, as in the seal of the State of Israel, the Menorah is also a revelation to man regarding how God works on the earth. It reveals His method to accomplish His desire in the earth.

According to God's instruction, the Menorah was designed after a plant (or group of plants) that are common throughout the Holy Land. These plants were well known by the nation of Israel and common during Old Testament times. Plants of the genus *Salvia* (Libiatae) likely were important in the design (Ex 37:17-24) of the Menorah. Plants of this family also frequently give off a strong fragrance that was likely used in temple worship as a part of the incense. Both aspects of the temple worship were ordained by God to play an important role throughout the history of Israel. This is true both from a practical aspect as well as from the prophetic.

When the nation of Israel stopped worship as a result of being scattered throughout the nations of the earth, the Holy Land (particularly the hills of Judah) continued to offer up praise and worship to God through the Menorah plants. The people were scattered but the land remained faithful and continued to offer up praise and worship throughout the years even to this very day.

The Menorah plants continue to grow to this day as they have over the centuries. When the hot daytime sun beats down on the landscape the winds carry the fragrance to heaven. Even to the end of the long dry season when most plant life is dry and brown the wilted and half curled leaves of the *Salvia* continue to give off a sweet fragrance, a reminder that even in the worst of times, even at the bottom of the valley, a sweet aroma is flowing to heaven. A reminder for us to continue giving off that sweet fragrance of love throughout those dry, parched times. One can still walk the hills of Judah and enjoy the smell of the air saturated with the fragrance of various species of *Salvia* plants as well as other aromatic plants of the region.

In Isaiah, God says He will never forget the land to which He is married. One reason God will never be able to forget His land is because the hills of Judah continue to produce a sweet fragrance and every time God looks to see where the fragrance is coming from He sees the Menorah plants (the plants are shaped like the Menorah) covering the hill sides of Judah. He is reminded by both the sweet fragrance and by the symbolism of the herbs and trees expressed in the Menorah of His eternal covenant with His portion of the earth. What a glorious reminder God prepared for Himself that He would never forget His land of promise. He planted a sweet perfumed garden all across His land that He would remember the charm of His bride. No matter what the condition of the land and people the sweet fragrance continues to rise to heaven and every time God looks down He sees His remembrances throughout the land. The Menorah was and still is a reminder to Israel to remember their God, but it is also a reminder to God to remember His people. God will never forget because the land speaks of the covenant!

When Jesus came, He called men to the kingdom of heaven and the dove was given as a symbol. The dove was given as a symbol of the Holy Spirit which Jesus received (The Holy Spirit descended in a bodily shape like a dove and abode on Jesus, Luke 3). Jesus now baptizes believers with the Holy Spirit in all fullness. As with the Old Testament symbols, the dove also represents what God is doing on the earth and how He is doing it.

The glorious "new thing" that God is currently doing involves the bringing of these symbols (aspects of His kingdom) together in Christ. Everything must come into unity under the authority of Christ, both in heaven and on earth (Eph 2:13-17). While Israel is the channel through which God will work, the Holy Spirit is the power to perform the work.

The nation of Israel was given the Menorah and the fragrant plants as a sign of the working of God's spirit on the earth. The church is given Jesus and the sign of the dove. The Menorah and the dove coming together represents the most powerful thing in the universe, the unity of heaven and earth in Christ which will totally restore the earth to its original created purpose.

We are currently living in the dispensation of the fullness of times and God is making the way for everything to come together from heaven and earth (Eph 1:10). The fig tree has budded (Mt 24:32-33) and God is grafting in all the branches. God is preparing Jerusalem for the return of Christ and the coming together of all things when heaven and earth will be united as God had planned in the beginning.

Jerusalem is God's capital city, and is becoming the focal point for the whole earth. The church started in Jerusalem. The disciples were told to wait in Jerusalem. The Holy Spirit first came in power to Jerusalem. The church spread from Jerusalem to Samaria and then to all the world.

Christ will also return to Jerusalem to receive His church, which we are told will be a glorious church. Christ is not coming back to receive an American church or even a gentile church, because the time of the gentiles is fulfilled. Israel has been grafted back into the vine and will become more glorious, because it represents the natural branches (Ro 11).

Christ is coming back in like manner as He left (Ac 1:11). Jesus left the beginnings of a new church in Jerusalem and He will come back to receive the completed church in Jerusalem. The former rains started in Jerusalem and the latter rains will complete the harvest in Jerusalem. The seed was sown in Israel, therefore the harvest must be in Israel.

Prophecy after prophecy talks about the glory of Jerusalem as Jesus rules from His city. Gentile nations will serve and give honor to Israel and Christ, Isaiah chapters 61, 62 and 66.

*Restoring Peace in the Holy Land

Another thing God is currently doing in the Holy Land regards peace. The ultimate goal of God is to establish righteousness and peace in Jerusalem (Isa 62:1). God's desire is for Jerusalem to be at peace and Psalms 122:6 reminds us to pray for that peace. We are also told to seek and pursue peace (Ps 34:14). Blessed are the peacemakers (Mt 5:9). God is now writing peace on the hearts of the people across the land. On recurrent trips to Israel this has been reinforced as people are asked throughout Israel to express their prayer requests. Almost without exception peace is at the top of the list, if not number one. Peace is first and foremost on the minds of people all across the Holy Land, both Arabs and Jews. In Ezekiel 36:37, God says, that when they ask of me that which I have promised I will do it. God is preparing the way to fulfill the desire of His heart in the land. However, God will establish peace in Jerusalem in His way and time and not according to men's ways or schedules. Many men have their own agendas for the region, but God has "the agenda".

Today, we hear much about peace in the regions around Israel and the whole world desires peace in the region except for a few extremists in the region bent on violence. But what kind of peace? Is the world seeking the peace of God or the peace of men? The two are very different and will bring very different results. God's view of peace requires obedience to Him and can only come as a result of His Holy Spirit working across the land as Jesus is lifted up. Men must first have the peace of God within themselves.

The peace agenda promoted by the spirit of anti-christ is also at work in the world today. The spirit of anti-christ has a pseudo-peace plan, one that will be accepted by men and nations void of spiritual understanding. Do not be deceived by Satan's plan because his pseudo-peace plan is in arrogant rebellion against God and will bring disaster to all who follow the deception. Satan always has a substitute plan based on deception and lies.

God's Peace Through Obedience

Israel's peace is determined by its relationship with God, not its relationship to other nations (Judges 2:20-23). Examples throughout Scriptures reveal that Israel always had trouble when they made peace arrangements with other nations and did not depend on God alone (Eze 29:7, Jer 42, Jer 17).

Man made political peace agreements have never worked. Today, every political peace agreement brings the region one step closer to disaster. Today's negotiated peace agreements are based on compromise after the desires, self-interest and greed of men.

Israel was never allowed to make agreements with other nations (Judges 2:2; Ex 30:32; Deut 7:1-5). Unmistakably God did not allow Israel to compromise with other nations. Why would God compromise with those who would try to destroy His plans, His land and His people? Particularly, why would God compromise with those whom He has totally defeated (Lk 11:16-23)? Is God so weak that He must compromise with man or nations (Isa 40)? No. In the Scriptures, compromise always resulted in judgement to those who compromised the things of God and will today also.

Compromise between Israel and other nations clearly go against God's declared eternal purpose and plan for the region. Nations and political powers must understand that God does not change his mind, compromise, or work with men in such ways. Men work as partners with God on the basis of obedience to His ways. Only those walking in the Spirit of God have the ability to understand His desires and what He is doing or will do in the future.

Peace in the Future

The question is not if Israel will have peace, but what kind of peace? Peace will come, but what kind of peace and at what price? Current peace agreements do not flow with the power of God's Holy Spirit. They are like salt water trying to enter a large, rapid flowing fresh water stream. Current peace agreements are for the most part in direct opposition to God's proclaimed plan for the region. Therefore, peace talks may only be different forms of the same age-old battle, only a deception to shift the conflict to another time and place. Something like this ..."if I can not win on the battlefield now, then perhaps I can win on the peace front until I can win on the battlefield?"

Guidelines for True Peace

The following guidelines must be understood and acknowledged before lasting peace can come to the Holy Land:
1. God has determined the borders of Israel. They will never change.
2. God has determined absolute authority over Jerusalem.
3. God has declared the Holy Land to be home to His flock.
4. God has declared the Holy Land to be His personal inheritance forever not man's.
5. Man has no authority over the land of promise or Jerusalem. It is God's alone.
6. Man must follow orders from heaven regarding Israel and Jerusalem.
7. Men and nations must give honor to Jerusalem, the holy land and pay tribute to it.

The shape and character of the Holy Land is not open to man's suggestions or opinions. Man has no authority to draw a map or work out a plan for the region. The plan has been worked out for many years. Man only makes the choice to obey or not to obey God's map and plan.

God's ultimate goal on the earth is to bring glory to His Name. This desire will be effectuated through Jerusalem and Israel. Peace can come only when men come under the authority of Jesus and are led by and filled with the Spirit of the Living God. Peace can come only through the Spirit of the Living God. Praying in the Spirit is the only hope for lasting peace because only Messiah Jesus can bring peace to Jerusalem and Israel.

Man's political peace initiatives involving compromise between nations are part of a great deception led by Satan's kingdom that will ultimately bring open rebellion against the kingdom of heaven. The result will be a declaration of war by God and a total destruction of earthly governments and kingdoms.

God's people may never compromise with evil. If only men could understand that when they walk in obedience to God they will be blessed and be given freely all the things they fight and kill to obtain in their own power.

Time for Heavenly Peace

O heavenly peace, now fill Jerusalem.
Peacemakers come and fill every home and street.
For this city shall be called the city of royal peace.

O mountains, cast off now every warmonger and evil tongue.
The horn of strange music and song has been cast down.
Music and voices of strange god's keep silent forever.

Tongues of peace and praise, break forth in royal color.
Speak loudly of the Prince of Peace.
People of peace come, fill every house, every hill and valley.

Messengers of peace, stand on the four corners of Israel.
Let the keepers of peace be stationed at every entrance.
Allow only the voices of peace to be heard in this holy place.

O Spirit of Peace, spread your wings over the holy city.
Blow heavenly winds of peace over the face of the land.
Carry the fragrance of peace to these holy hills.
Prince of Peace, take your place in Jerusalem.
Engrave Jerusalem with your graving of peace.
Only the God of Israel shall receive praise in this place.

Pray for the Peace of Jerusalem (Ps 122:6-9)

"Pray for the peace of Jerusalem:
they shall prosper that love thee.
Peace be within thy walls, and prosperity within
thy palaces. For my brethren and companions'
sakes, I will now say, Peace be within thee.
Because of the house of the Lord
our God I will seek thy good."

When we pray for the peace of Jerusalem we pray for much more than peace from conflict in the Middle East region. In reality, we are praying for the Prince of Peace to come and establish His heavenly kingdom in Jerusalem. Also, we pray for the new Jerusalem, the heavenly one that Jesus went to prepare (Jn 14:3); the Jerusalem that Paul called the free Jerusalem; the mother of us all (Gal 4:26); the Jerusalem that Abraham looked for whose maker is God (Heb 11:10); the Jerusalem that John saw coming to earth (Rev 21:10). Jesus is the only one who can bring real lasting peace to Jerusalem, because He is the only one who can bring peace to the hearts of men and establish righteous authority over Jerusalem and at the same time destroy the works of Satan on the earth. Jesus is clearly the only one who can fulfill the request of this prayer for peace and prosperity in Jerusalem. We must pray for the peace of Jerusalem, justifiably the world can not be at peace until Jerusalem is at peace.

Psalms 122 does not limit our prayers or place our hope on some man made peace, but on the true heavenly peace through the return of Jesus. We must pray for Jesus to return and graft all the branches into the vine and bring salvation to Jerusalem. The chapter goes on to talk about prosperity (vs. 6 and 7), and only the blessings of God's kingdom can bring prosperity to the earth. Only then will God rest and the whole earth receive blessings and the joy of the Lord. Pray for the sake of brethren and companions that Jesus comes and sets up His kingdom, that all the world, both Jews and gentiles will be blessed and prosper. Pray that righteousness will fill the earth.

*Removing the Covering from the Earth

Another marvelous thing God is doing in the land is prophesied in Isaiah 25:7, *"And I will destroy in this mountain the face of the covering cast over all people, and the veil that is spread over all nations."* The covering will first be removed over Israel. This will open the door for the glory of the Lord to return to Jerusalem. The departure of God's Glory is described in Ezekiel 11:22-25. However, in Ezekiel 43:1-5 God reveals that the glory of God will return in like manner.

At some point in time, the veil over all the nations of the earth will also be removed. As the veil is removed from the nations of the earth, they will see Satan's deceptions and understand the purpose and glory of Israel. Believers should see and understand now because we are instructed by the Holy Spirit, and nothing can veil the power of the Holy Spirit!

Once the veil is removed all nations will understand the following truths:

1. That Israel is a blessing to every nation (Ge 12:3).
2. That Israel is a witness of God (Isa 43:10).
3. That Israel reveals God's glory (Isa 46:13).
4. That Israel is the seat of God's glory
   and authority (Jer 33:23-26).
5. That Israel is God's channel to reveal himself
   and His will to the world (Ps 103:7, Ge 1:3
   and Isa 43:10; 21).

Nations and people need to understand that their actions and attitudes towards Israel and the "House of Judah" are actions and attitudes towards God. Those that reject Israel, reject God; those that despise Israel, despise God. On the other hand, those who bless Israel also bless God.

This blindness towards Israel is a part of the veil that causes nations and people to view Israel from a carnal, natural point of view and therefore miss God's divine plan and purpose for the nation. As a result, many nations and people bring judgment upon themselves because of their dealings with Israel.

Israel in many respects represents God on the earth and most people miss that concept. However, the concept is not new, God told Abram, *"I will bless them that bless thee and curse him that curseth thee"* (Ge 12:3), and Jesus said, if you have seen Me you have seen the Father (Jn 14:9). Jesus also expressed the same concept when He said that you can not hate your brother and love God! We can not reject those that God has sent and claim to love God (1 Sa 8:7)!

In God's view, Israel is the glory of all the earth (Isa 60; 61:5-6). Therefore, once this veil is removed and people see the truth, the response of the nations will be love and appreciation (Isa 60:9-10). The nation and people of Israel will be praised by all nations of the earth (Zep 3:19-20).

*Engraving His Graving on His People

A fourth marvelous thing God is doing throughout His land is engraving His graving (Zec 3:9) upon His people, *"behold, I will engrave the graving thereof, saith the Lord of Hosts, and I will remove the iniquity of that land in one day."* God will engrave the Spirit of the living God upon His land and people.

Zerubbabel was made a signet, a seal (Hag 2:23), that again at this time God would stir up the Spirit of the people as they obeyed Him. Again, today as in the time of Zerubbabel, God will work in the Holy Land by His Spirit to accomplish His desires.

"Not by might, nor by power, but by my Spirit,
saith the Lord of hosts." Zec 4:6

Has now God taken the plummet in hand and prepared to make every mountain against Judah a plain (Zec 4:7-10)?

Master Engraver

O Lord, take in hand the chisel and hammer.
Engrave your graving upon your holy mountains.
Let your engraving be as the seven eyes.

Take your plummet in hand and finish this house.
That your engraving will run to and fro over the earth.
That all may rejoice at the work of your hands.

What God does in the Holy Land He will do by His Spirit. *"Not by might, nor by power, but by my Spirit, saith the Lord of hosts" (Zec 4:6).* This was the word of the Lord to Zerubbabel and it is also the word of the Lord regarding Jerusalem today. Zerubbabel was made a signet (a seal) regarding the second coming of the Messiah (Hag 2:23).

In some respects, Israel represents a unique aspect of the Holy Spirit ministry. We see this in several areas:

1. The land is God's personal possession and as a
   result He takes a personal interest and a
   special hands on approach to the region
   Deut 32:4, Zec 2:12).
2. We are told in Scriptures that He will accomplish
   His work by His Spirit (Zec 4:6).
3. We are told to pray for the Holy Land. Prayer
   is a spiritual weapon (Ps 122:6-9).
4. The purpose of what God is doing in the Holy Land
   is to bring Glory to His name.

Perhaps like no other place on earth, men must be led by God's Spirit to do His work in this region. Everything must be done in God's perfect time and way. He has a perfect blueprint and time line for the region.

God's work in the land is also difficult and even dangerous. This is the land that has killed God's prophets throughout the ages and even Jesus himself.

Yet, what a marvelous place to work in union with the Holy Spirit and see the manifestations of God as He prepares the way for Jesus. The fullness of God's glory and power is given to this region to do His work.

Nothing can stand before those anointed to do His work in the land. All the powers of darkness and all the armies and powers of earth are nothing before the mighty power of God's Spirit moving over the land to complete His purposes.

It is awesome to walk under that kind of anointing and experience that kind of authority to do the will of God. It is the kind of anointing that makes the powers of darkness be at rest and the desires of evil men be as nothing, the kind of anointing that makes whole cities subject to God's pleasure and stilled from doing harm to His anointed. What a glorious thing to see God's heavenly messengers take authority over whole cities on behalf of His servants.

Who would want to live any way other than by the power of the Spirit of the living God, doing the works of God as an obedient servant without fear, just trusting God. Is not that the pattern that Jesus demonstrated?

Jesus started the Church by the power of God's Spirit. Everywhere He went the spirits of religion wanted to kill Him, yet He walked and worked in their midst with peace and authority. God's Spirit will finish the Lord's work in the Holy Land in the same way and with the same anointing and power.

What God is doing is by His Spirit. The only way to function is in total obedience to the Holy Spirit, no other way will work. Man alone has no power to work in the Holy Land. This area is becoming the battle ground of spiritual kingdoms with powers far greater than man can understand. Only the Spirit of the living God can alter events in this region of the world. Only as God's servants work in total obedience to Him will they be able to effect the master's design.

Today's Mountains, Tomorrow's Plains

Great arrogant mountain before Jerusalem.
Your heights appear so foreboding to men.
Your peaks are like knives and spears.

You are fallen before the Lord God Almighty.
Your great heights shall be made a plain.
Your sharp peaks shall fill the valleys.

Come down, O mighty heights and sharp peaks.
Earthquakes shall shake your foundations.
Jerusalem, high and lifted up, shall look over you.

Gentleness shall rule over you like a lamb.
Peace shall make her home in your pastures.
Jerusalem shall be your keeper and maker.

Arise, O Lord of Hosts, look on your city.
Establish your sanctuary in greatness.
Let your mercy flow like a mighty river.

*King David's Eternal Kingdom
Jeremiah 33:19-22

Additionally, God is in preparation to fulfill the promise to King David that his house, his kingdom and his throne would be eternal. God is currently preparing the earth for this eternal reign of splendor. Therefore, a foreshadowing of this kingdom must come into being along with the nation of Israel in preparation for the return of King Jesus. We currently see the manifestations of this fulfillment in at least three areas: one, prophetic anointing; two, the coming physical kingdom; and three, the throne of authority.

Prophetic Anointing

A channel is being opened in the land for the people to hear God and receive God's instruction. The change parallels differences between the prophetic orders of Eli and of Samuel. God is removing the curse of silence from the land and again speaking to the land and the people.

Eli's sons ministered in vain because they knew not the Lord nor did they hear from the Lord (1 Sa 2:3). However, the word of the Lord came to Samuel and he ministered God's word to the nation.

God is now again raising up prophets in the land that can hear God after the order of Samuel in preparation for the return of David's Kingdom and the return of Jesus. This is a very significant event in God's timetable of events in the Holy Land because David's anointing came through the prophet Samuel. It was not until a change in the prophetic order that God could speak to the nation and that David could be anointed king and his kingdom established in fullness.

God is confirming the reordering of the prophetic by raising up men in the Land that can hear His voice and by raising up the land of the prophet Samuel. As a symbolic witness, two related things are currently taking place on the land of the prophet Samuel; one, part of the area is being developed as a tourist site by the government and two, another part of the land is being developed by believers. Both of these concurrent events bear symbolic witness to a new prophetic anointing on the land in preparation for the eternal kingdom of David.

Events currently taking place in Israel and on the land of the prophet Samuel represent awesome prophetic signs that reinforce the expectations of the soon return of David's kingdom and the coming of the Messiah. These events signal that the prophetic anointing is already flowing into the Kingdom of David. Therefore, in the spiritual realm, the kingdom of David currently exists in Jerusalem.

A Physical Kingdom

The second sign of the anointing that is going forth to prepare the Kingdom of David is expressed in the prosperity and blessings on the land of Israel. David's kingdom was very successful and very prosperous as demonstrated by his son Solomon. The prosperity and blessings will be multiplied many times over in the new kingdom.

Authority

The third area in which we see the kingdom of David being established is in the region of authority. God is giving the State of Israel authority over the promised land and the City of Jerusalem. The conflict in the region today is the same as in the time of David. God will again bring Israel in authority over the land as the Kingdom of David is established. In Old Testament times it was not until David was anointed King by Samuel that Israel gained authority over Jerusalem and the land of Israel. Today, that authority is being established and will be completed within the throne of David as Jesus establishes His heavenly rule over Jerusalem.

Powerful events are taking place in the Holy Land as God releases the anointing of His Holy Spirit to establish the fulfillment of King David's house in Jerusalem, His kingdom in Israel and His throne over all the kingdoms of the earth. The visual establishment of God's promise to King David in the Holy Land is an awesome prophetic sign as to the times in which we live and how close we are to the return of Jesus to earth.

Chapter 4

GOD'S PROPHETIC TIME CLOCK

"For the Lord's portion is his people; Jacob is the lot of his
inheritance. He found him in a desert land, and in the
waste howling wilderness; he led him about,
he instructed him, he kept him as the apple of his eye."
—*Deuteronomy 32:9-10*

When we study Scriptures, we see the importance of understanding what Israel represents as well as what Israel does not represent. Israel is not just another nation on the map inhabited by just another group of people. Israel is not to be called common, taken lightly or passed off as unimportant. Israel demands consideration and respect because God demands consideration and respect.

Man cannot escape from the reality of Israel anymore than man can escape from the reality of God. To ignore Israel is like ignoring God. God requires that believers take an active role regarding Israel. As with all aspects of the kingdom of heaven, if we do nothing we receive nothing and as a result remain servants of Satan's kingdom.

These concepts are important because, as we will see later, nations have been judged by God simply because they spoke of Israel as common and did not understand Israel's divine anointing and purpose on the earth. They did not understand that God's hand is always on the nation of Israel and that men and nations receive from God's hand either blessings or curses depending on their actions.

Israel the land, Israel the nation and Israel the people are unique upon the earth because God said it was to be that way. Israel is an earthly nation but clearly with a heavenly mission and anointing. All that man may do and say will never change God's design and purpose for His nation because Israel is at the center of God's eternal plan for the earth. God's covenant with Israel is eternal and He has promised to always protect and watch over the land and the people. God will use all of His vast resources to see that His will and purpose for Israel is completed right down to the last word. As a result all who come against Israel will have to answer to the one Lord God, the God of Israel.

Israel and its people are God's chosen instruments to work out His plan on the earth that His glory be revealed. The selection of Israel by God was not based on the merit of the people but on God's divine wisdom and purpose. Plainly, it is not the place of the gentile nations or any man to question God's wisdom. Obedience to God's desires alone brings blessings (Dt 28). We are told we have the mind of Christ, therefore we must come to see things as God sees them (1 Cor 2:16). We must view Israel as God does and understand His divine plan and purpose. God views everything from the viewpoint of the kingdom of heaven and so must we to be in unity with Him. That is possible only as we are taught by the Holy Spirit. Currently, the whole earth is veiled regarding Israel and God's plan. The only way to see through that veil is by the power of the Holy Spirit. Without that revelation anointing of the Holy Spirit we cannot see or understand things of the kingdom of heaven (1 Cor 2:14). Only when God lifts that veil over the earth will nations and people be able to see and understand Israel and God's plan. God only reveals the gems of His kingdom to those who are worthy to receive. For example, God reveals things to His friends (Isa 41:8 and Ge 18:17), Jesus used parables to hide the truths from those in darkness (Mt 13:11) and the Holy Spirit is our teacher (Jn 16:13-15). The Holy Spirit is given to those who love God (Jn 14:15-17). Those outside the kingdom do not have the Spirit of Truth (Jn 14:17) and cannot see and understand spiritual wisdom.

Israel continues to be a sign to the whole earth of what God is doing. Israel is a lesson from the past, a sign to the present, and a prophetic revelation for the future. The land of Israel is like a great time piece that reveals God's timetable on the earth regarding heavenly events.

In many respects Israel is like a great living blueprint that reveals God's building plan to men. The nation is in fact a dynamic blue print that is being constructed daily as new revelations result in additional understanding of how God deals on the earth. For believers, Israel is also a step by step guide as to what God desires of His people as they become partners in the building of His kingdom.

Israel is also a standard for judgment for all people, including nations, individuals and the church. In many cases, the nation is a stumbling block to the rebellious and proud. On the other hand, Israel is a standard of blessing to the humble that listen, hear and obey the voice of God.

God uses the marriage relationship to describe His love for the land and its people (Isa 62:4 and Jer 3:14). This marriage relationship also expresses the unity and oneness between God and His chosen land. God's relationship with Israel reveals a great deal about God himself, His desires, His loves and the way He views things. This marriage relationship also illustrates to us the commitment, and protective covering God has placed over the holy land.

God and Israel are one, they can not be separated, consequently when we bless Israel, we bless God. The converse is also true. The way in which people and nations respond to Israel reflects directly their relationship with God.

Blessings and curses are given to individuals, groups and nations on how they relate to Israel. Time and time again God makes it plain that blessings and curses from heaven are given regarding obedience or the lack of obedience (Dt 28). God told Abram *"and I will bless them that bless thee, and curse him that curseth thee: and in thee shall all families of the earth be blessed"* (Ge 12:3).

In Deuteronomy God told Israel that he would put diseases on all that hate Israel (Dt 7:15). Clearly destruction waits at the door for those who hate Israel (Isa 17:12-14; 49:26, 51:23 and Jer 12:14-17). On the other hand blessings wait for those who bless Israel. In Deuteronomy the curses are given to destroy those who are disobedient (Dt 28:20). All of these same curses will fall on those that hate Israel, that they be consumed by destruction.

Israel offers believers a unique opportunity to bless God. Today we have a special opportunity because the Jewish people live in the Holy Land. Therefore, we have the unique opportunity at this period of history to bless the land, the nation, and the people all at the same time. We are living in a unique season of time with great opportunities like few generations of people have had. Yet, we must take advantage of these during our window of opportunity. If we miss this, how great will be the loss of blessings and also the judgment for not listening to God when He spoke.

Prophetic Signs

Psalms 19:1-3, *"The heavens declare the glory of God; and the firmament sheweth his handywork. Day unto day uttereth speech, and night unto night sheweth knowledge. There is no speech nor language, where their voice is not heard."* Throughout the ages, God has revealed His ways through various means; examples include signs and wonders, sometimes by angels and other times by prophetic revelations. Today Israel is one of those signs, a very important and momentous sign to all nations and peoples of the earth. Isaiah 11:12 says, *"And he shall set up an ensign for the nations, and shall assemble the outcasts of Israel, and gather together the dispersed of Judah from the four corners of the earth."*

God reveals His way only to those with ears to hear and eyes to see (Ps 19:1-4). Jesus did that which was revealed to Him of the Father and He told His disciples that the Holy Spirit would show them all things and things to come (Jn 16:13-15). God continues to show and speak the things of heaven this day to His people. Currently He is speaking in many ways through Israel. Repeatedly, the message goes forth from the Holy Land in many forms.

For example, a very interesting and yet very powerful sign of the times, as well as an important revelation regarding God's working on the earth, is coming out of Israel in the form of a dove. Throughout the history of the earth the dove has been used by God to teach. It has also been used as a symbol of various events and workings of God.

Again today, the dove is becoming a very notable world wide prophetic symbol regarding the times in which we live and impending events on the horizon of time. Interestingly the dove is currently appearing on many things throughout Israel. Both as a tourist attraction, from pins to sweatshirts, and also as a national peace symbol on many official government tourist materials. One of the first things many tourists received in recent years when coming to Israel was a road map with a dove on the front. As a result tourists from all nations of the earth take these prophetic symbols from the holy land back to their nations as a witness of God's glory. These symbols speak a prophetic message about what God is doing in Israel to the entire world.

The prophetic significance is however complex. The dove symbol involves multiple aspects of God's moving in the Holy Land, and also points to the end time rebellion and the rise of the end time satanic religion. Yet, all aspects center on one central theme, Christ's return to earth. For example:

First, the dove symbol is a sign that peace can come to the Holy Land only by the anointing of the Holy Spirit in God's time and way. In addition, world peace can come only through Israel because all blessings and authority go out from the Holy Land.

Second, the dove is a sign that the latter rain anointing of God's Holy Spirit is already flowing over the Holy Land. The oil of anointing is currently flowing throughout Israel to make final preparation for Jesus and His kingdom on earth.

Third, the dove is a sign that all Israel will be saved, will acknowledge Jesus as their Messiah and will be a witness of God. As such, it is symbolic of perfect unity and fullness. For many, the dove is just a simple sign of peace, but in reality the dove symbol represents much more than that because the "Prince of Peace" is Jesus. The dove is considered by many in the church to be a sign of the Holy Spirit, because *the Holy Ghost descended in a bodily shape like a dove* (Lk 3:22). In John 14:16 it says that Jesus is the one who sent the Holy Spirit to earth to abide with believers, and the Holy Spirit gives glory to Jesus (Jn 16:14). Also, the Holy Spirit will engrave Jesus upon all the house of Judah (Zec 3:9).

Throughout the Holy Land (and all the world) the dove symbol is proclaiming that Jesus is the Messiah of Israel and that God's Holy Spirit is currently working in the land to execute His perfect plan. Furthermore, it is significant that the dove symbol is being used on many official government items. As a result the State of Israel is proclaiming both that Jesus is the Messiah to the whole world and that it is time to prepare for His return. Israel is assuming her role as God's witness to the earth.

Fourth, the dove is a powerful prophetic sign that a "new thing" is approaching. In Genesis 8:8-12, the dove was sent out to find new life so that a new generation of men could go forth and populate the earth. The dove was to bring back a sign that God had prepared the new season and the time was at hand for events to take place. The dove is an indubitable sign of impending transition on the immediate horizon.

Again today, the dove symbol is going forth to typify an approaching new season. Even more significant for this generation is that the dove indicates that this "new season" is even now at hand. In Scriptures, the dove appears just prior to a major event. For example, the dove abode on Jesus just prior to the start of His public ministry, also the dove was sent out to find an olive branch just prior to Noah leaving the ark to repopulate the earth.

Fifth, in Isaiah 60:8, the dove is associated with the gentile ministry to Israel. As the dove symbol goes from Israel throughout the world, it reminds gentile nations everywhere that they have a responsibility to Israel because it is God's Holy Land. God has not changed His mind, and now is the time for fulfillment of the vision.

Sixth, in Ezekiel 7:16, the dove is used as a symbol of the mourning remnant of Israel. Today a remnant is being raised up in the Holy Land to mourn for the nation in preparation for what God is going to do in the land. Ezekiel 36: 37 says that when the people ask, then God will hear and do what He has promised. The remnant is now asking and seeking God! Can the answer be far away?

Seventh, the dove symbol is an important reminder that encompasses many of the things God is doing in the Holy Land as He prepares the earth for His reign. The dove is a reminder to all people of the earth that soon heaven and earth will be united under one great kingdom as Jesus returns as He promised (Jn 14:3).

The False Dove

While the dove symbol is used by God in both the Old and New Testaments, Satan has also used it to represent his working. As Satan often does with holy things, he has taken the dove and created a counterfeit image to confuse the truth.

We must remember that the dove (often with the olive branch) was worshiped by the Babylonians and was a part of the idolatrous Assyrian worship (Hislop, 1916). Since the old Babylonian worship of Nimrod is being revived in preparation for the end time events, it is not surprising to see Satan also using such symbols today throughout the world.

Specifically, the dove is a symbol of God's perfect peace, but it is also being used today as a symbol of the world peace designed and directed by Satan. This is that false peace that will deceive the earth. This false peace being developed by men and nations represents an impending false security that will result in swift divine judgments

(Reference: Hislop, Alexander, 1916, The Two Babylons on the Papal Worship, Loizeaux Brothers, Inc., Neptune, N.J. Pg. 78-79. 1959 Edition.)

on a deceived world system. The false dove image thus represents a false pretense, a demonic peace which is in reality a rebellion against the kingdom of heaven.

Shophar

Isaiah says, *"for out of Zion shall go forth the law, and the word of the Lord from Jerusalem"* (Isa 2:3). Jerusalem is God's city and is the place that His word always goes forth from, why should it be any different in these end times? One of the great signs of the times we see and hear around us is the blowing of the shophar in Jerusalem and throughout the world. As the nation of Israel is a sign of the end times so is the blowing of the Shophar.

In Scriptures the Shophar is associated with the glory of the Lord and sounds just prior to God's glory being demonstrated on the earth. For example when the walls of Jericho fell down the nation of Israel was marching around the wall sounding the Shophar and carrying the Ark of the Covenant. The Shophar represented the voice of God while the Ark of the Covenant represented the physical presence of God's glory. What a powerful combination! As God's glory was released the walls came down and victory was given to Israel. Also, in Exodus chapter 19 the voice of the Shophar is associated with the demonstration of God's glory.

Is not the sounding of the shophar today in Jerusalem also the announcement of some great event getting ready to happen? In Luke 21:24 Jesus said, *"and Jerusalem shall be trodden down of the Gentiles, until the times of the Gentiles be fulfilled."* In 1967 Jerusalem stopped being trodden down by the gentiles and the age of the gentiles came to an end. As the sound of the Shophar was heard in Jerusalem the announcement sounded loud and clear to prepare the way of the Lord to return.

Joel says, *"Blow ye the trumpet (shophar) in Zion, and sound an alarm in my holy mountain: let all the inhabitants of the land tremble: for the day of the Lord cometh, for it is nigh at hand"* (Joel 2:1). Joel confirms that the blowing of the shophar will signal the return of the Lord. Today, the shophar is being sounded throughout Jerusalem, Israel and the world. As the shophar is taken from Israel to the various parts of the earth the voice of the Lord is being heard announcing the return of Jesus.

God says in Jeremiah 6:17, *"I will set watchmen over you saying, Harken to the sound of the shophar."* Today, also we need to hear and listen to the voice of the shophar as it speaks a clear word from the Lord God of Israel to all that will listen. Today, the sound of the Shophar is saying many things to those with an ear to hear, for the trumpet is loud and clear.

Additional Prophetic Signs

Other signs of the times include the Jewish people gathering into Israel from the four corners of the earth, and Ephraim and Judah living together in peace as brothers (Isa 11:12-13).

The changing character of the land is also a sign, as the desolate places become inhabited with gardens and fenced cities (Eze 36:35). The government of Israel is a sign to the nations (Hag 2:23). Jerusalem exhibits many prophetic signs as the city continues to develop and become a world center of banking, commerce, and culture. The entire country and the people are confirming prophetic signs to the nations of the earth as to what God is doing across the earth in this day.

Full Anointing on the Land

Lord let your olive trees grow strong.
Let the tender branches be many
and let them produce an abundance of oil laden fruits.

May each tree produce an endless flow of pure oil.
That your golden lamps will burn brightly without dimness,
continually producing the brightness of your glory
as a continuous witness throughout all the earth.

Let your pure oil flow in fullness divided seven ways.
Only let each of the seven be in fullness as the one,
that each flame will have your undivided anointing.

Emerging Markets

The current world wide phenomenon known as emerging markets is interesting in light of Scriptures regarding Israel. This is associated with new national freedoms, free trade agreements and general world prosperity which also appears to be related to end time events. These events are all synergetic and propelling the world towards God's divine plan. This combination of events will result in a great, widespread increase of accumulated wealth in nations throughout the earth. This is a part of the end time events that God has designed and will use to fulfill prophetic revelations regarding Israel.

This wealth is being accumulated by God to bless Israel. In God's plan, the gentile nations will become a great storehouse of wealth so that many blessings can be transferred to Israel. Israel will not have to earn it or work for it, but it will be given to them from the gentile nations. We see these prophetic Scriptures in places such as Isaiah 60:5, *"because the abundance of the sea shall be converted unto thee, the forces of the Gentiles shall come unto thee;"* Isaiah 60:11, *"that men may bring unto thee the forces of the Gentiles;"* Isaiah 60:16, *"Thou shall also suck the milk of the Gentiles, and shalt suck the breast of kings;"* Isaiah 61:6, *"ye shall eat the riches of the Gentiles, and in their glory shall ye boast yourselves."* These Scriptures all speak of the transfer of wealth from the gentile nations to Israel. God will accumulate and store the wealth of the earth in the gentile nations and then it will be given to Israel when he determines the time is right. This transfer of wealth is a part of the gentile ministry to Israel as we see in Scriptures such as Isaiah 60:8-11 and 61:5. For example Isaiah 60:10 says, *"And the sons of strangers shall build up thy walls, and their kings shall minister unto thee."*

Those who continually try to scare people by talking about the destruction of the global financial system are for the most part just speaking a bad report. This kind of talk for some reason seems to make some people happy. Certainly, all the world systems are going to be destroyed in God's time, but only for the purpose of bringing glory to His name. These kinds of destruction will happen in various places at various times, but not on a world wide scale, until God says it is time for the completion of His program. Those who say it is imminent any day do not understand how Israel fits into the global system.

We must understand that this is a time of great change and turmoil resulting in many problems throughout the earth. However, as we proceed into the end times, prosperity will continue to increase until catastrophic events bring an end to man's dreams. This end time prosperity is a part of the deception that will cause people to continue following after the ways of Satan until it is to late. Like the tower of Babel in Genesis 11, or the flood in Genesis 6:7. It is essential to understand Scriptures, not what men say. Those who followed after religious doctrines of men have always been wrong.

Chapter **5**

GOD'S INHERITANCE

*"Prophesy therefore concerning the land of Israel, and
say unto the mountains, and to the hills,
to the rivers, and to the valleys, Thus saith the Lord God;
behold, I have spoken in my fury,
because ye have born the shame of the heathen:
therefore thus saith the Lord God;
I have lifted up mine hand,
Surely the heathen that are about you,
they shall bear their shame."*
—*Ezekiel 36:6-7*

Israel is a nation, a people and also a region of land. Israel is a special land for which God determined the borders many years ago. He has set it aside for His chosen purpose. This land area called Israel is unlike any other place on earth because God selected it as His personal possession. He has a special interest and purpose for this unique section of the earth. This land called Israel will bless the whole earth and bring glory to His name. Possession was determined a long time ago and is not up for review. Yet, today the conflict continues over possession of His Holy Land. Many claim possession, but God calls them tongue waggers (Eze 36:3) because He has given it to His flock (Ge 15:7).

The Whirlwind

O heathen, why do you proclaim possession of Israel
Would you steal from God?

O enemies of God, listen Now,
Have you not heard; have you not understood.

Israel is the land of God's flock,
Jerusalem is the holy city of the Lord of Hosts.

God's holy prophets long ago prophesied your ruin,
Your vain professions blow in the wind.

O tongue waggers who proclaim possession,
Your words are scattered in the whirlwind.

The words of the God of Israel stand strong,
His words are forever established in Mt. Zion.

The special nature of this land of Israel is revealed in the way God speaks about and directly to the land. In Scripture, God speaks directly to His land in a personal and loving manner. He speaks to the land and it's various aspects such as the hills, valleys, rivers, just as he would to a person and they respond. He also told His prophets to prophesy to these features of the land in the same way, and they have responded.

We see God's special interest in the land and its hills and valleys in the following Scriptures: Deuteronomy 11:11-12, God says He careth for the land and His eyes are always upon it; In Leviticus 26:42, God says He will remember the land; and in Isaiah 62:4, God states that He is married to the land. In God's view, marriage reflects a loving and everlasting relationship. God says the marriage relationship can only be broken by death. Since God will never die, Israel will always be His partner in a covenant relationship that will never change.

In the book of Ezekiel, we see examples of Gods instruction to His prophets regarding the land. God told His prophets to prophesy directly to the land in Ezekiel 36. Ezekiel gave the land instructions (Eze 36:8) and also gave a prophecy regarding it's future (Eze 36:9-10). Today, believers should also be prophesying the desires of God to the land, for these things are examples and lessons to us as God's children so that we can carry out His desires in our day.

Specific Instructions Regarding Prophecy

Ezekiel in chapters 34-37 gives us important guidelines (examples) for speaking prophecy regarding God's land and people. These examples include prophecies against people and nations, prophecies of blessings, prophecies and instructions aimed directly to the land, and instructions to the people and specifically the nation of Israel. These prophecies are given to fulfill God's desires towards the land of Israel.

In some examples, these prophecies reflect the attitudes and actions of various people toward Israel and reveal God's response. Consequently, these specific instructions are in fulfillment of God's promises to treat people and nations on the basis of their treatment of Israel. It is important to understand that the same holds true today regarding the land and people of Israel.

Prophesy Against Evil Leadership

Ezekiel was told in chapter 34 to prophesy against rebellious leaders that were benefiting themselves at the expense of God's people. Today God has given us the same tools as well as the same responsibility to bring down such strong holds of Satan through prophecy.

How long will God sit in heaven and watch evil men rebel against his commands? Shall self-exaltation and pride be tolerated forever? Shall not the humble prophesy and those that are greedy towards brothers find desolation? Shall not those who put on the robes of pride be found naked and those who rob the flock be in want of a flock. For now is the time for the righteous to prophesy to the wicked. The cup of wickedness is filled to overflowing. The watchman must now speak forth to the sons of evil so that wickedness will be cut off from the land forever. Let the men of evil desires and speech be put outside. The wicked shall flee in seven ways at one word from the Lord of Hosts.

Then the watchmen shall prophesy blessings and goodness, and righteousness and praise shall fill the land. Healing shall flow to all men abundantly and mercy and blessings shall be like green grass throughout the land.

The Oppressors

From your seeds of evil,
you shall eat the bread of disaster.
From your fruits of hate,
you shall drink the wine of wrath.
From your rivers of rebellion,
you shall drink the bitter waters.

For all that you have stolen,
shall become garments of rags.
For every bushel filled with grain,
shall have seven holes.
For every house,
shall come seven varmints as associates.

When you reach for a blessing,
a curse shall fill your hand.
When you speak a word of peace,
confusion will return.
When you seek rest,
the earth will quake and roll.

The Friends of God

From your seeds of mercy,
you shall eat of the bread of life.
From your fruits of love,
you shall drink the sweet wine.
From your rivers of obedience,
you shall drink of quiet waters.

For while you rest in peace,
new garments shall overtake you.
For every bushel of grain,
shall seven be added.
For every house,
shall flow the sound of children and joy.

When you reach for blessings,
seven shall fill your hand.
When you speak a word of peace,
understanding shall flow.
When you seek rest,
all will be at peace.

Prophesy Against Rebellious Nations

In Ezekiel chapter 35, Ezekiel was told to prophesy against Edom because they were oppressors. Today many nations oppress Israel and claim possession of God's land. Any person or nation that claims possession of any part of Israel is stealing from God and soon becomes His enemy. Believers today as in prior times should be actively prophesying God's desires against nations that are present day oppressors of Israel. As God's watchman, prophesy against these evil nations; destruction will overtake them from heaven.

Nations of Oppression

Nations of greed and pride listen to the holy one of Israel,
Because you make my people desolate crying will overtake you,
All your plans of hate and evil will come upon you seven fold.

The water of life will dry up in your land unto desolation,
Drought shall fill your table as a vast storm,
All will wonder in amazement at the speed of your destruction.

Your fields and pastures shall search for fruit,
From the West and the East shall come a whirlwind,
From the North and the South, the seasons shall be confused.

Your best cities shall howl from misery in every quarter,
Brother shall seek brother, but none shall find wisdom,
Every blessing shall be as the wind that was yesterday.

God sits in the heavens with complete authority over earthly matters. Oppressor nations will have no choice but to watch Israel prosper and receive great blessings while they are over taken with destruction (Isa 17:12-14, 49:26 and 51:23).

Prophesy Blessings to Israel

In chapter 36, Ezekiel was told to prophesy to the land of Israel, to the mountains, the hills, the rivers, and valleys, as well as to the cities.

Today, we are seeing these prophecies being fulfilled daily. In Zechariah 10:1, we are told to ask in the time of the latter rain and the Lord will give abundance. Now is that time! God expects His watchmen to keep speaking to the land of Israel that His blessings can flow over the whole land. Through prophecy, we take an active part in being partners with God's working on the earth. Just as men have been instructed to prophesy to the earth throughout history, God expects believers today to do the same thing. Now is the time for believers to prophesy blessings and fulfillment upon the Holy

Land, the nation, and the people. As the watchmen prophesy to the dryness, God will bring life to the Holy Land as Ezekiel was shown in chapter 37.

Prophesy Jubilee to the Holy Land

Prophesy Jubilee to all the land and inhabitants
of God's glorious resting place.
Prophesy to all the Holy Land and the people of Israel
fullness of freedom.
Prophesy to all the land, mountains, hills, rivers and cities
fullness of restoration.

Mountains of Israel, hear your God and ring forth
with triumphant freedom.
Shoot forth with splendor the fullness
of your bountiful possessions.
Prepare the way for the return of God's family
from the ends of the earth.

Hills of Israel, rejoice in the return of your lush
emerald green pastures,
For thou shalt resemble the Garden of Eden
with every good and beautiful thing.
In majestic freedom, call forth the abundance of your
new found possessions to cover the earth.

Valley's of Israel, look upon the peacefulness of the
crystal clear waters that abound.
Pure waters, flow profusely over the whole land of Israel, may life
and peace arise in every section.
Living waters, flow full and freely throughout
every valley with life giving blessings.

Rivers of Israel, take from your deep source the
living waters of restoration.

Flow freely throughout the whole land,
that life and joy will fill every valley to overflowing.
Living waters, bring abundant living grace
to everything that is in your path.

Holy land of Israel, receive and rejoice in your
glorious freedom and restoration.
Your possessions will shine as magnificent jewels
to the nations of the earth.
Your eternal family shall always be at peace
and rejoice in the one God of Israel forever.

Prophesy to the People

In chapter 37, Ezekiel was told to prophesy to the "House of Israel". Today we must also prophesy to the "House of Israel", that they would be filled with the Holy Spirit of God and be given new life. If God will not rest until peace fills Jerusalem, how can His servants rest until the job is finished? We must continue to prophesy blessings to His people and land.

Men of Wisdom

Come, men of wisdom and understanding,
those who have the Spirit of the living God of Israel.
Come, men of counsel and might and those with knowledge
and the fear of the Lord.
Come and be established in God's holy eternal abiding place.
See joy flow from every house.

Holy Spirit, come and spread your wings over God's blessed
people that they will stand and live.
Holy Spirit, blow the breath of life over a desolate people and land
that your lush gardens will spring forth.
Holy Spirit, speak peace and gladness into the land that men
everywhere will praise the God of Israel.

Prosperity, flow over the inhabitants of the land
that all would drink of your waters of blessings.
Peace, rest over the house of Israel
as a gentle dew over the landscape on a fresh summer morning.
Blessings of goodness, fill each home with joy,
afresh with the opening of each new day.

Men of Israel, arise and be filled with new life and fullness.
Be filled with the fatness of God's rich, chosen land.
Drink deeply of the Holy Spirit of the living God of Israel.

God has told us that it is by His Holy Spirit that He will bring to pass His plan for His people (Zec 4), *"Not by might, nor by power, but by my spirit, saith the Lord of hosts."* Paul tells us in Romans 11:31-32 that it is through the gentiles that Israel will receive His mercy, *"Even so have these also now not believed, that through your mercy they also may obtain mercy. For God hath concluded them all in unbelief, that he might have mercy upon all."* As believers speak forth in the manner shown us in Ezekiel chapter 37 and prophesy to the dead bones and to the Holy Spirit, God will perform His mighty works.

God hears His watchmen as they prophesy after the desires of His heart. As believers in Jesus prophesy against evil leaders and evil nations, and at the same time prophesy goodness to the Holy Land of Israel, God will move with great power to complete His holy plan. Believers will be blessed to have been partners with God in this great work.

Now is the Time to Speak

Speak, holy children, chosen of God,
hold not still at such a time as this, but speak freely.
Speak forth prophecy to the Holy Land of Israel
after the heart of God.

Speak, for God has ordained His people to speak
as He did the holy prophets of prior days.

Speak, for now is the time to send forth
the desires of the most high God of Israel.

Speak blessings and prophecies that
His Holy Land would hear and live.
Speak rivers of anointing from His holy place
that His pleasures be done before all men.

Speak to the apple of His eye
to fulfill its chosen eternal destiny of splendor.
Speak forth with power the desires of God,
that the whole earth may see and live.

Speak forth, that the holy spring will flow with the waters
of life and the trees will bud and be fruitful.
Prophesy, children of the Most High
to the mountains, hills, valleys and rivers of Israel.

Prophesy restoration to the whole house of Israel
and let the veil be removed from the earth.
Prophesy blessings, mercy, joy and all the fullness
of the Holy Spirit to all the house of Israel.

Believers have received the golden sceptre (Est 5:2), and should be partners (Est 5:6) with God in what He is doing in the land today. A part of this partnership involves a responsibility to prophesy God's instruction and desires to the Holy Land in the name of Jesus. God wants His people to call forth the land to resurrection life. Part of the job of making straight the way for the return of the King of Kings is speaking to the land: arise, be resurrected, put on the royal garments and be prepared to meet King Jesus!

The Holy Land will be blessed beyond measure. Israel will become the most beautiful and lovely place on the earth, even like the Garden of Eden (Eze 36:35). Each of us has been given a partnership in the process, yes, even a responsibility!

Hills of Praise

O holy mountains of Judah, arise with singing and praise;
The Lord Jehovah hath placed His foundation in your midst.
The whole earth waits to rejoice in your beauty.

O hills sing forth with mighty praises;
Welcome the cities of God's holy people of praise.
Come people of praises, prosper and rejoice in beauty.

O living waters, spring forth from His holy mountains;
O mighty spring, break forth from under the sanctuary.
O trees of life, spring forth from the great valley.

O songs of Jehovah, break forth over every mountain;
Cast off every strange song and voice, sing to Jehovah.
Songs of Israel, fill the mountains and valleys of Judah.

O holy mountains, dance to the songs of His people;
Let heavenly music alone break forth over the hills.
Let only the Lord of Hosts be praised in this place.

O songs of praise, break forth in mighty power;
As the Holy Spirit calls for a song of homecoming.
O eternal rejoicing and blessings, flow forth now.

The Land Called Judah

As the mountains of Jerusalem are the home of God's Holy City, so then the mountains of Judah are His garden. Has not God placed a special blessing and given a special anointing upon the Judean landscape around Jerusalem? These hills around His holy city will receive a special blessing as God restores perfect harmony between the heavens and His earthly creation.

Judah is the land of milk and honey (Ex 3:8 and 12). Beyond milk and honey, the land will be the glory of all lands (Eze 20:6) and will receive many blessings (Eze 36:6-12). The land will be as the Garden of Eden (Eze 36:35) and enjoy every blessing in all aspects of both the living and physical environments, for God does all things well and in perfection!

The land of Judah will become home to prosperous cities and have a super productive climate. The region will be blessed with pools of water and inhabited by every good plant. A multitude of animal life will prosper there. It will reflect the perfection of God's creation.

Now is the time for God's people to speak blessing upon the land. Already the land is being blessed by the Spirit of God in fresh new ways.

End of Mourning in Judea

Mountains of Judea, break forth as a prosperous garden;
Shoot forth with the vigor and beauty of a new creation.
Mountains, let every flower and fragrance excel in splendor.

Holy hills, be clothed with a green carpet of grass and reeds;
Provide abundant homes and peace for every good creature.
Men of praise, come now and prosper among God's garden.

Abundant rains of blessings, flow upon His holy mountains;
Trees and flowers, come forth in every kind of royal splendor.
Every creature, come and rejoice in the new found blessings.
Valleys, let pools of clear pure water abound in your midst;
Every valley and hill side, exhibit royal color and glory.
Lord, rejoice at the beauty of your restored garden.

North wind, come in your season of blessing;
South wind, come in your season of blessing.
Blessings, come forth, in all seasons from all corners.

The Place Called Jerusalem

In the flesh, with our natural eyes, we see a city trodden down by men from many nations, a city that is left desolate (Mt 23:38). However, in the spiritual realm we must see the city that Abraham saw (Heb 11:10), the city that Paul talks about in Galatians 4:26, the city we are told to pray for in Psalm 122, and the city shown us in the late chapters of Revelation.

The city we see today is an instrument in the hand of God to purify and refine the earth, a city that will be a strong mountain against the ungodly and bring in the fullness of righteousness and glory.

Jerusalem is an awesome place because the Lord God of Israel is an awesome God, and Jerusalem is His personal chosen portion of the earth (Zec 2:12). The Lord God of all the universe said that he will not rest until righteousness and salvation fill Jerusalem (Isa 62:1). Surely God will not rest while men are attempting to complete their desires with His holy city. Can the church of Jesus Christ continue to sit back and be unconcerned about God's holy city in a time such as this? Believers need to start viewing the city from a spiritual perspective and understand the region from God's point of view.

God will use whatever is required of His colossal power and authority to completely protect His purpose for Jerusalem. As the greatest King that this world has ever known prepares His place in Jerusalem, all the resources of His vast universe will focus on His holy city. Anything that comes against God's eternal plan for Jerusalem will be totally destroyed. Only a complete fool, or a person who is totally deceived, would contend for God's holy city. Satan and all those who follow him, men or nations, will be destroyed over the controversy for Jerusalem. God has said that he will defend, deliver, and preserve the city (Isa 31:5). Would men attempt to steal from God?

Jerusalem is again today becoming the focal point of spiritual activity, as heaven and earth focus on the holy city. God is working His plan for the earth through and from Jerusalem. As a result, He is increasingly manifesting His glory through Jerusalem. At the same time, the city is increasingly becoming the center of spiritual conflict as we approach the end of this age. The controversy over Jerusalem is bringing into focus the conflict between righteousness and evil in Israel and specifically in Jerusalem. God is currently preparing the way to send His righteousness out from Jerusalem to all the earth. At the same time, Satan is attempting to fill the city and land with the fullness of evil. Powerful demonic forces are moving over the city and land in preparation for the great conflict that waits on the horizon. The old prophets of Baal are again flowing over the land and stalking the city like an evil tide as they prepare for their great destruction in the valley of Jezreel.

Jerusalem is a city of extremes: evil and righteousness, prophets of God and prophets of Satan, a place of joy, peace, and comfort or pain, evil and conflict. For example, Jerusalem is a city of bondage and yet freedom, of judgement and righteousness, of controversy and peace, of comfort and fear, of holiness and evil, of faith and atheism and a city of totally defiled religious traditions (Jews and Gentiles) and yet those who walk by the Spirit of God (Jews and Gentiles). A marketplace of the worst and the best daily coming and going from its gates. Paul in Galatians chapter 4 refers to the two Jerusalems. One, that is under the bondage of the law (the one the world sees in the flesh), and the other that is the free Jerusalem in Christ. Now is the time of transition when both covenants are inhabiting the same place at the same time as God prepares to bring His heavenly kingdom into place.

A Veiled Jewel

Currently the glory, character, and purpose of God's Jerusalem is veiled to the world (Isa 25:7), but when that veil is removed the whole earth will see the marvelous glory of the city. There will be great joy and praise unlike anything this earth has ever experienced as the new Jerusalem is revealed in its fullness. Then people will fully understand Jerusalem. However, today Jerusalem is still in bondage to the law (Gal 4:25). Jerusalem remains as Jesus described the city in Matthew 23:38, *"Behold, your house is left unto you desolate."* As a result every kind of varmint and defilement has come in under the veil and filled the city as well as the land of Israel. Again today, as in the time of Jesus, Israel is revealing the true nature of those who walk under the law and defilement of sin, a clear demonstration for all to see of the defilement and hopelessness that comes from religious tradition and man's religious systems. Jesus was well aware of the outcome and warned the people continually about the emptiness and destruction that would follow those who would choose tradition over freedom in Christ (Mt 15:6-9).

When one visits the city today the moral state of the land appears as described by Zephaniah in chapter 3 verses 1-7. One sees a nation filled with every kind of sin and witchcraft. Zephaniah calls the land filthy and polluted, full of oppression, full of disobedience and rebellion, full of unbelief, a nation that has forsaken God, princes are as roaring lions and their judges are as evening wolves: prophets are treacherous persons and priests have polluted the sanctuary; crime is common; violence and corruption are everywhere. This was just what God said would happen (Dt 28) to those who rejected the truth. The end result of man's religious traditions.

However, God is preparing the way for all this to change as he brings salvation to the nation Israel (Ro 11:25-32). In Galatians 4:26 we see another Jerusalem, a Jerusalem of faith, a spiritual kingdom. This will replace the current Jerusalem when Jesus returns. This is the city Abraham looked for (Heb 11:10) and the Jerusalem we are told to pray for (Ps 122). The glory of God is again coming to His holy city of Jerusalem (Eze 43:1-5).

In spite of many catastrophic events occurring in Jerusalem, modern day Jerusalem is still a miracle. God is preparing to complete His plan for Israel that His name be glorified. What we see currently is only an initial start of what God has planned for His Holy City. This city will be filled with such abundance of glory and blessings that only time will reveal the full scope of God's plan. God has taken a special interest in Jerusalem and will mandate that the resources of the whole earth be used to bless His city (Isa 60:8-11; Rev 21:24-27). We are currently seeing a shadow of things to come in the heavenly kingdom.

Jerusalem remains holy in God's view, a marvelous place that will be blessed beyond anything this earth has ever experienced. Believers must learn to see through the veil and view Jerusalem in faith. As a result, those who believe, seek the holy city, obey God and bless Jerusalem will be blessed in many ways (Ps 122; Isa 66). Jerusalem is a comfort and blessing to all those that love the city.

A City Named By God

Names given in Scriptures for Jerusalem foreshadow the future Jerusalem and are therefore important. Ancient names for God's city include Ariel (Lion of God) and Salem (Perfect). The Bible uses a great variety of other names also to describe the city: City of God, City of the great King, Throne of God, Holy Mountain, Holy City, City of Truth, The Lord is there, and The Lord our Righteousness. Future names during the reign of Christ include additional names: My Delight, a Green Olive Tree, Holy Mountain, City of Righteousness, the Faithful City, Sought Out, Zion of the Holy One of Israel, plus others. Currently the city is starting to take on these characteristics as a sign of the times and as a clear prophetic sign to the nations of the earth.

Jerusalem is God's delight. Surely anything God delights in will be most glorious. If God delights in the city, so must those who are one in unity with God. Therefore, believers must also delight in the city and seek to be a part of what God is doing. Are not believers His workmen and partners in His working on earth? Our understanding and response to Jerusalem must reflect an understanding and practical application of the many names God uses to describe His holy city. If believers claim to love God and claim to be His bride how can they not be excited about Jerusalem at such a time as this? In a marriage relationship both partners have to be excited about and working towards the same things for there to be unity and peace in the relationship. God is excited about Jerusalem and what is being prepared in heaven, therefore, His bride must also be excited about the things of God.

God is preparing the city as His holy habitation on this earth and its temple as His holy oblation in preparation for earth and heaven to be united under the authority of King Jesus. God is excited about His son, Jesus, coming back to Jerusalem to establish the kingdom of heaven in the holy city. Jesus is also excited about coming back to Jerusalem, because this time He will be king in His city. The Holy Spirit is also excited about heaven and earth coming into unity. Are you excited about Jerusalem? Can you hardly wait to go there or get back over there to see what God is doing? Every believer should be!

Jerusalem is far more than just a city or a location on some map. The city is in reality an awesome and fearful place when one considers God's view of the city, past events that have occurred in Jerusalem, future events that will occur and God's plan for the region. The Holy Land is scheduled to become a centerpiece of His majestic Kingdom. The holy city should inspire a solemn reverence and at the same time an excitement in the heart of every believer like no other place on earth.

The Holy City

When holy fires envelope you, out of the flames flow an endless array of heavenly colors that encircle you as a covering of golden silks enlightened by clear pure white light.

When you rest at peace, the beauty of perfect stillness transcends your highest hills and angelic music fills the hills as the sound of a thousand harps descending as sparkling white dew kissing the waiting landscape with a breath of life.

How great and yet fearful are you upon the earth.
A holy city that encloses both alpha and omega,
yes both life and death.
Your walls and gates are an everlasting sign
to all the nations and kings of the earth.

Your shadows reveal the fullness of righteousness and judgment.
The fullness of destruction is spilled out of your midst
and yet you await the glory of untold restoration.
Fear and peace pass each other at your gates.

Magnificent city, let your true word reach to the ends of the earth.
All the nations will be humbled at your foundation and yet will
be blessed by the living waters that flow from your depths.

In spite of the great controversy and seemingly arrogant boldness of God's enemies to possess the holy city for false gods in Satan's name Isaiah 31:9 says the nations around will be discomforted and afraid of the ensign, *"and he shall pass over to his strong hold for fear, and his princes shall be afraid of the ensign, saith the Lord, whose fire is in Zion, and his furnace in Jerusalem"* (Isa 31:9). Clearly we are starting to see the fullness of this Scripture today as the nations of the region and of the earth are discomforted and fearful of what God is doing in Israel and Jerusalem. For those who are in Satan's camp, God's ensign is an ominous event on the horizon of time.

The Great Controversy

The cries for peace are heard throughout the whole earth.
Pursuits of peace fill and consume the nations of many lands,
Yet peace rides on the whirlwind of an endless storm.

Everywhere peace stands in the earth and shouts for honor.
Peace declares its glory throughout the heavens;
Peace is proclaimed from heaven and earth by men and angels.

Yet, the fruits of peace remain hidden among the forest trees
Clouds of earthly vapor hide peace from many seekers
Sounds of this life mute the voices of peace and reason.

Pseudopeace encamps around the holy city as wolves in white,
Crying, peace, peace, let us have peace on our platter.
Watching every gate for an evil opportunity to destroy.

Prophets of Baal are released from long held tombs to cry peace.
They walk the land and city and search every home and office.
Like a plague of Locusts, they seek every living thing for a hearing.

For all shout peace with a left hand of fellowship;
They strike with peace in the night like a scorpions tail.
The plague of this peace is as a tornadic cloud over the land.

The great controversy rages over Jerusalem today as it has for thousands of years. Great nations and Kings have come to Jerusalem only to discover that the city is God's alone and He determines the city's present and future. Yet today, the city remains full of controversy as Satan continues in his attempts to deceive men and nations.

Only the curse of deception can explain man's obsession to rule Jerusalem. Yet, it is difficult to comprehend anyone or nation wanting to claim possession of Jerusalem, because clearly anyone or any nation (outside of Israel) that claims possession of Jerusalem fights against God's plan for the city. As a result, they are up against all the vast power of an immeasurable, eternal universe. Because the city is God's personal beloved possession. The time is approaching when everything and everyone who is against God's plan for Jerusalem will be totally destroyed in a day as Jesus himself comes with the armies of heaven to claim full possession of His Father's city and His throne. The awesome power of God has been recorded in Scriptures and demonstrated throughout history to accomplish His will on earth, but nothing has ever been observed to compare with the glory, power and destruction that will be used to claim Jerusalem and restore His will for the region.

However, let not the church sit at ease in self-righteousness because God is always judge and never spares unrighteousness. Not only is the holy eternal city of Jerusalem a place of judgment for the rebellious nations of the earth but it is also a city of judgment for religious hypocrisy. Jerusalem is a standard of refinement and purity on God's terms and is therefore a city of judgment for the church as well. Was the "old religious" system of Jesus' time spared during the destruction of Jerusalem? For does not judgment begin at the house of God (1 Pe 4:17)? Just as the nations of the earth have an appointment in Jerusalem, so does the church. Just as God is going to restore the earth to its original unity with heaven so is He going to restore the church to its original unity as demonstrated by Jesus and recorded in the early chapters of Acts. Remember, *"judgment must begin at the house of God"* (1 Pe 4:17). The church can have unity with God only as it is shown all things and led by the Holy Spirit. The church started in Jerusalem, it spread from Jerusalem, and Jesus said He would return to Jerusalem. Jerusalem is, always has been, will continue in the future to be the center of God's activity and authority. The glorious omega church will be centered in Jerusalem.

However, the church that Jesus will accept must be pure and righteous. Anything that comes into holy Jerusalem must be free of abomination and all defilement (Rev 21:27). God never changes and is therefore always righteous. That which he receives must also be pure and righteous including the church that Jesus comes to receive. God has revealed through His people and prophets that often the purification and restoration process is a refining process. In Isaiah 31:9, Jerusalem is described as a furnace of fire. God will not allow any dross to remain in His true church.

Interestingly, Jerusalem is currently calling many segments of the church back to its roots from all regions of the world. Yet, many of these various segments come to Jerusalem bringing all the dross and defilement with them: idolatry, witchcraft, arrogance, pride, jealousy, fighting, self-glorifying and self-exaltation along with many other ways of religious men. They come speaking vanity and their right hand is a right hand of falsehood (Ps 144:11). God will rid himself of these strange children.

God is not bringing these gentile ministries to Jerusalem to save the city. He will do that by His Holy Spirit through love and mercy. Would a righteous God allow His Holy City to believe such defilement and curses of man's pagan religious systems?

Jerusalem is calling many in the church to its refining furnaces. God will demand that His Omega church be pure and giving glory only to Jesus. Jesus will not let anything of man's fallen nature contaminate His Holy City.

God will move with great power over Jerusalem in the fullness of time, but He will do it in His time and by His Holy Spirit as He moves through those individuals He has refined and chosen for this work. He will use those who demonstrate the fruits of the Holy

Spirit because that is the real test of abiding in the vine. God requires love, unity and good fruit.

True believers (friends of God) can rejoice to remember that Jerusalem is a place of comfort and peace for the righteous that seek her (Isa 66). No other place on earth can bring the kind of comfort, blessings, and peace that Jerusalem can. As believers join with Jerusalem, they join with God in a unique relationship because God has a special relationship with His Holy City. God's presence is in Jerusalem and His heavenly messengers continually come and go from Jerusalem. This special heavenly attention creates a special spiritual anointing and presence in the region. Also, the region is close to the heart of God, so those that take a special interest in Jerusalem and develop a love for the region gain a unique relationship within the family of God.

The city is unique in that it calls those whom God has chosen to His Holy City to come. However, this call to Jerusalem is by invitation of the Holy Spirit. As Jesus called the early disciples, so today the Holy Spirit is calling a people that will learn and obey. Those who hear the call must be as the disciples and make a commitment to the heavenly Jerusalem above all else. They must also be as the great witnesses in Hebrews 12:1 and be persuaded, embrace and confess (Heb 11:13) the city of God that they look for in faith (Heb 11:10).

Holy Spirit Blow a Gentle Breath Over the Land

Holy Spirit blow, from the four corners
upon the still, golden, resting embers.
Blow the winds of life, over the resting embers,
so that they will glow and sparkle afresh.

Spring forth flames of life and burn out the dross,
that only pure unleavened holiness will light the Holy City.
Burn bright and hot upon these golden nuggets,
so that they will shine as pure heavenly gold.

Jesus clearly demonstrated the preeminent principle of being led by the Holy Spirit during his walk on earth. Jesus was anointed with the fullness of the Holy Spirit during His time of earthly ministry. He made plain His total dependency upon the Father through the Holy Spirit for everything. He did nothing (Jn 5:30), said nothing (Jn 6:63), or revealed nothing (Jn 7:16-19), except what was shown Him by the Father through the Holy Spirit. Is not this the essence of perfect unity, perfect dependency? Clearly, righteousness for believers comes only from unity with Jesus. It is also true that perfect unity with Jesus can come only through full and perfect dependency upon the Holy Spirit whom Jesus sent from the Father (Jn 16). Jesus said the Holy Spirit would show and teach believers all things (Jn 16:13-15).

The Holy Spirit gives glory only to Jesus. The Holy Spirit manifests only the fruits of the Spirit - perfect love! Anything that does not give glory to Jesus alone is not of the Holy Spirit (Jn 16:13-14)! Anything that does not come from the Holy Spirit is rubbish and will be destroyed by fire because it is not pure. Only that which is pure will be accepted by God. Only that which is pure and holy will be allowed into the Holy City of Jerusalem. Pray for the city of Jerusalem and rejoice with it. Be a part of what God is doing to make straight the way of Jesus in the Holy Land.

Glory of the Ages

O Jerusalem, His glory shines on you like a circle of fire.
Let your inner midst by filled with eternal brightness,
For the Lord of Host is a wall of fire around you.

Prepare a dwelling place for the King of Kings O Holy Land.
His eternal majestic glory shall take rest in your midst,
Sing aloud, for you are chosen the apple of His eye.
The mountains of Judah alone are an eternal inheritance.
The horns that scattered you are all cast down forever,
Let your horn arise over the earth in royal splendor.

Be silent all nations, come and worship in Jerusalem,
Observe the glory that shines in His holy mountains.
Let all the earth sing and rejoice in the Lord of Hosts.

Jerusalem and the Great Holy Spirit Fires

A great end time outpouring of God's Holy Spirit is coming upon the earth. An outpouring of anointing like the earth has never observed. A time to fulfill the latter rains so that the harvest will be overflowing. Currently, an anointed people are being prepared for this great event.

However, it is not the outpouring that is popularized today in the Christian media. It is not the outpouring that gentile churches talk about and attempt to bring about by the ways of men to glorify men.

Most gentile ministries are looking for a move of the Spirit to build their self-made programs and bring glory to men's ways and human appointed leadership. God is far above this kind activity and always brings destruction to this kind of pride.

What God does always brings glory to His name. What man does brings glory to men. This world wide anointing of the Holy Spirit upon the earth will flow out of Jerusalem, God's capitol city, as did the former rains. From Jerusalem, the rains will go out to all the earth with such power and anointing that all will know without any doubt that God is one-hundred percent in control of events. As with Pentecost, the Holy Spirit will do the acts and men will explain and call others to repent, believe and walk in holiness. It will flow out from believers called to Jerusalem for this purpose and anointed by the Holy Spirit to take the living rivers of God's word throughout the earth.

God will not revive the old traditions of man's kingdom. He never has before! He will do a new thing with a new people that walk in true love, seek first the Kingdom of God, and are in unity with Jesus and walk in the power of the Holy Spirit.

Only those set free in Christ by being totally dependent on the Holy Spirit can please God and do His true work. Like the mighty river that will flow from the temple in the new Jerusalem, this river of anointing will bring life to all that drink from its waters (Eze 47).

Chapter 6

A Rose Blooms

"For the nation and kingdom that will not serve thee
shall perish: yea those nations shall be utterly wasted."
—*Isaiah 60:12*

When Israel became a nation in 1948, a very important global event occurred that changed the world forever. This event probably had more profound long term influence on men and nations than any other single occurrence since the life of Christ. Israel becoming a nation again initiated the time of fulfillment of the gentile nations, and God's clock of earthly events again begin to focus around the physical nation of Israel. The time of fulfillment was constituted in 1967 when Israel gained control of Jerusalem (Lk 21:24), *"and Jerusalem shall be trodden down of the Gentiles, until the times of the Gentiles be fulfilled."* As these world changing events unfolded, the generation of change emerged throughout the world as God's plan for fulfillment took on new meaning. Israel was grafted back into the vine and, as Paul notes in Romans chapter 11, the original branches will be more glorious than the wild branches. In 1988 the generation of change received a new emphasis as Israel entered its second forty year time period (God often dealt with Israel in 40 year time periods). Many world changing events have taken place since 1988 as God is now doing a "new thing" with a new emphasis.

Nature teaches us that grafts require a season of time to become established. The newly grafted branch does not bud, flower and set fruit until a following season. Over the years of this current generation, the world has watched this process take place and now the branches have become established and are starting to flower (second 40 year period). When a tree flowers, the fruits are not far behind, always within the season of that generation (Mt 24:34-35). As a result of this progressive process, the earth is a very different place today and is continuing to change rapidly as God releases His power and anointing into the new branches. The anointing and glory of God is again returning to the land of Israel. This is having a profound influence on the entire world as does any situation that causes a major shift of power and authority.

Israel is God's chosen servant and as such the nation must be prepared for the special mission that God has ordained for the land. Isaiah 43:10 proclaims that mission as being God's witnesses, *"Ye are my witnesses"*. Israel is to witness that God alone is Jehovah and that there is none other (Isa 43:10-12). Israel will also shew forth God's praise (Isa 43:21). God's great and eternal glory will be revealed to all nations and people through Israel and specifically Jerusalem.

As God prepares Israel for the fulfillment of this mission and the return of Jesus to earth, world events will be oriented to focus on the fulfillment of this desire of God. As a result God's magnificence and all powerful glory is going to be manifested in the days ahead with fresh exalted power. The nations and peoples of the earth are going to know that before God's power they are less than nothing (Isa 40:12-17). All the military power of all the nations across the earth is a small thing to God. His word will prevail perfectly in all things.

Currently, we are seeing this focused working of God being manifested in an increasing number of aspects as He brings to completion prophecies and desires regarding Israel. As a result, the world is in a rapid transition mode and is entering a time when alterations will continue to intensify as we get ever closer to the return of Jesus and the time for God's kingdom to take control of Jerusalem (Isa 40:3-5).

The following are among seasonal changes that will continue to have a major influence on the world as God deals with men and nations in preparation for His heavenly kingdom. We must remember that in the heavenly kingdom, Jerusalem will be the center of all authority on earth.

1. God's attention is focused on the Holy Land of Israel again (specifically Jerusalem). National and world events must relate increasingly to Israel and God's working to complete his plan for the region.

2. God's time table of world events is now worked through and towards Israel. In order to understand world events one must understand what God is doing with the promised land (His land) and the "house of Judah". Nothing happens independent of God's desire for the land of Israel.

3. Nations are increasingly dealt with regarding their response to the nation of Israel. God views the treatment of Israel as synonymous with one's attitude towards him. God is always with Israel! Those with God's blessings will be those who bless Israel (Isa 41:11-12). Those against Israel will be God's enemies and receive total destruction.

4. Spiritual power and authority are moving from the church in the gentile nations to Jerusalem. God's glory and anointing is returning to the land. The church of Jesus Christ started in Jerusalem and everything will end in Jerusalem. Along with this process, the churches in the gentile nations will become increasingly apostate and antagonistic towards Israel, the two frequently compliment each other.

5. Israel's role in world events will continue to increase until they become the center of world attention and conflict. Then finally, the nations of the world will be ruled from Israel.

6. The nation of Israel, and specifically Jerusalem, will increasingly become a world capital. This world influence will include all aspects of business, culture, science, power, authority, beauty, and wisdom. The greatness of Solomon's kingdom was only a shadow of the new Jerusalem. What God is building in this generation is a sign to the whole earth and a shadow of His eternal city and plan for the earth.

The Nation of Israel in the World

God's kingdom and Satan's kingdom are at war (Lk 11:16-23). As a result, God's nation, Israel, is also at war with a world system currently influenced by Satan, *"the prince of this world,"* (Jn 12:31). The conflict taking place in and around the Holy Land has been taking place for thousands of years and must be understood in the context of a war between spiritual kingdoms. The kingdom of God is currently being established in Jerusalem even while His enemies are encamped all around the Holy City.

Israel, as a nation, must always depend on God (Jer 17:2-7); anything short of that is a sin. However, God sometimes uses His people to bless and carry out His will. For example, in recent years God has used His spiritual nation (the church) to protect and bless Israel. This has been particularly important during these years of establishment and growth. Believers will continue to play a part in the development of Israel and preparing the way for Christ up to the time He returns.

Psalms 122:6 says, *"they shall prosper that love thee."* This conditional blessing is an eternal law of God. This law was first expressed to Abraham when God told him, *"And I will bless them that bless thee, and curse him that curseth thee: and in thee shall all families of the earth be blessed"* (Ge 12:3).

This law is repeated in the Old Testament (Isa 60:12) and confirmed in the New Testament (Ro 11; Lk 7:1-10). Jesus endorsed this concept in a story in Luke chapter 7. When the elders of the Jews came to Jesus beseeching him to come and heal the centurion's servant, they told Jesus he was worthy because he loved Israel and had built them a synagogue. Jesus confirmed this by going with them and blessing the centurion, healing his servant. Jesus observed he was a man of great faith but his faith had already been demonstrated by his kindness to Israel. This law also follows on into the millennium (Isa 66:10-14).

It is critical that we understand this concept as one of sowing and reaping because it still applies to the world today. Our response to this truth will have great influence on both our private and national vitality.

We do not bless Israel because we feel like we should, or because it makes us feel good or because the people are particularly good or righteous (because, outside of Christ, they are not). We bless the Holy Land, the nation of Israel, and the Jewish people out of obedience to God. We also bless the house of Israel because we love God and want to be a part of His workings on the earth. Deeds are done by faith that such acts of blessings will produce fruit in God's way and time to His glory.

Our blessings need to be directed toward the Holy Land, the nation of Israel, and the house of Judah but we do it as unto the Lord for the purpose that His name be glorified. Scriptures teach us that God's working and purpose towards Israel is to bring glory to His name (Isa 48:11; Eze 36:22-24, 32). Therefore, we bless God's land and people by faith in their unbelief that they will believe (Ro 11:31-32) and through their belief, God's glory will fill the earth.

It is important that people and nations understand that blessing Israel has no relationship to what the people believe, the moral state of the nation, how they treat others, or even their relationship with God. Our treatment and response to Israel has nothing to do with our feelings towards the house of Israel, but rather our relationship to God. We serve God, not Israel! God's command is non-conditional and independent of visual parameters. We always respond to God's desires by faith. The purpose for mercy and blessings are solely to bring glory to God, not men or nations. Blessings on Israel are simply a response of obedience to God. Like in the Garden of Eden,

God gives no explanation, just a command to obey for the good of all concerned. God has all wisdom and knowledge and is under no obligation to explain His ways to men. Man's obligation however, is to obey! Therefore, acts of obedience may or may not have any direct immediate relationship with the gospel of Jesus Christ. Israel will believe when the Spirit of God moves over them, not in man's determined time or ways. Zerubbabel was told, *"Not by might, nor by power, but by my Spirit, saith the Lord of Hosts"* (Zec 4:6). This is the way God always works, and this word of the Lord still applies to every situation today.

It is also helpful for gentile believers to comprehend that the reasons for blessing Israel have nothing to do with the nation or the people being better than any other nation or peoples. God is not a respecter of persons, but selects people and nations for His purposes. God selected Israel for His glory.

God does not save people because they are good, but in His loving mercy. Each person is saved by grace through faith, not of good works. We must remember this when dealing with Israel, because none of us would be saved if salvation depended on our goodness.

The future promised salvation of Israel is the same. God will save Israel out of his great mercy, that his name be glorified. Today, the nation of Israel, is full of every kind of sin and defilement, much like Jesus described Jerusalem in Matthew 23:38, *"Behold, your house is left unto you desolate."* The nation is totally desolate from a spiritual perspective. This desolation has created a vacuum that Satan continues to fill with every kind of defilement. Throughout the land is found every kind of extreme ranging from religious self-righteousness and dead traditionalism to every kind of defilement and total denial of any God. Yet, God will use the nation to bring glory to His name and in one day all will believe.

Time to Listen to the God of Israel

Throughout history God has given instruction regarding His will for His people as well as warnings to those who would speak against or harm His chosen servants. Today, Israel is God's servant, therefore, those who reject Israel in reality are rejecting God, because those who reject God's servants are rejecting the God who sent them. Just as those who rejected Samuel in place of a king rejected God (1Sa 8). Clearly those who would be an enemy to the house of Israel would also be an enemy to God and will receive His promised judgments kept in store for those who plant such seeds. (Isa 17:12-14; 49:22; 51:21; Jer 12:14; 25:15-28; Joel 3:2-8, etc.) Any people would be foolish as a nation or as individuals to disregard God's instructions and warning in respect to Israel. Not only out of fear of judgement but also out of fear of missing the blessings associated with being a friend of Israel and as a result also a friend of God.

Joel 3:2-8 speaks of the judgments, of those nations that have offended Israel. They will clearly reap the harvest of that which they have sown. The nation of Israel will in the years ahead prove every nation on the earth to see where they stand regarding obedience to God. As we continue to approach the day of Christ's return to Jerusalem, the whole world will increasingly focus on this small but very important section of earth called Israel because, it is God's special place. As a result the battle between God and Satan will center over Jerusalem as God prepares to destroy the power of Satan over the nations of the earth. Jerusalem is a city of great glory, but it is also a city of great judgment that will weigh the nations of the earth in its balance.

Deuteronomy 32:43 says *"Rejoice, O ye nations, with his people: for he will avenge the blood of his servants, and will render vengeance to his adversaries, and will be merciful unto his land, and to his people."* Nations and people make a choice to either rejoice with Israel and be a part of what God is working in the land or to fight against both Israel and God (Isa 66:10). Those who strive and war against Israel shall perish and be as nothing (Isa 41:11-12). God, who hates lukewarmness, will not allow neutrality (fence riding) because each individual will tip the balance in one direction or the other.

Ezekiel chapters 25-29 contains a series of prophecies against gentile nations. It is significant that in each example the reason God proclaims destruction upon these groups of people is their mistreatment of Israel and the house of Judah, some for only speaking against Israel, and others for dealing against the nation in various ways. God requires respect and honor be given to His nation and people.

God has not changed His mind regarding Israel nor do I believe He has developed more tolerance for the enemies of Israel. As in the past, those who speak or deal against Israel will have to pay the price for their actions because by doing so they have become the enemies of God.

The examples listed below are given to us as a warning against such actions (either in word or deed) and also on the positive side, as an encouragement to be a friend of Israel and receive God's blessings kept in store for those who would be on God's side.

Ammonites (Ezekiel 25:1-7)

The Ammonites were glad to see the temple profaned, to see the land of Israel destroyed and to see the people go into exile (25:3). Not only were they glad but they rejoiced by clapping their hands and jumping for joy because they despised the land of Israel (25:6).

They did not understand that by these actions they were revealing their attitude towards the Lord God of Israel. They rejoiced to see God's enemies victorious over God's chosen people and land. If the opportunity had arisen, they would have done the same thing to God himself!

Today also, there are many that despise the land of Israel and the Jewish people. Even within the Christian church, there are those with this attitude. No doubt God has reserved for these His cup of wrath. However, the friends of God will pray for Israel, bless the land, and extend mercy to the house of Judah.

Moab (Ezekiel 25:8-11)

Moab said that Judah was like all the other nations. Therefore, along with the Ammonites, they received God's judgment.

Unfortunately, we hear this same idea expressed today. Even within church circles that claim to be servants of the Lord God, these kinds of ideas are expressed in both word and deed.

However, in God's view, the Holy Land of Israel, the nation of Israel, and the house of Judah are all very special and have special anointings resting on them. Throughout Scriptures, God makes it plain that He has a very special eternal relationship with the land of Israel (Ge 17:1-8; Lev 26:42-43; Dt 11:11-12; Isa 62:4 and Joel 2:18). God has chosen and set aside the land and its people for His special purpose and for His glory.

Understand, that Jerusalem has many functions in God's plan: Jerusalem alone is God's holy city, Jerusalem is God's eternal earthly capitol and has been sanctified by God for the special mission of bringing heaven and earth into unity under Jesus. Israel is holy unto God, therefore, the land and people are not to be regarded as or called common or unclean. Peter was told in Acts 10:15, *"What God hath cleansed, that call not thou common."* When man takes lightly or disregards that which is holy, he is in danger of judgment. God did not agree with Moab that the land and nation called Israel were like the gentile nations. God likewise does not agree with those today who would say that Israel is nothing special (just another nation); or that God has cast off the nation of Israel and no longer has a special interest and anointing over the Jewish people and their land; or that God has replaced Israel with the church (Jer 51:5; Ro 11). Do not be deceived by such teachings and ideas spread by false prophets. The salvation of Israel is an everlasting salvation (Isa 45:17). God's promise is an everlasting covenant. He will give Israel all the good He has promised (Jer 33). Every word ever spoken by God is eternal and will be as He said!

In Jeremiah, God's relationship with Israel is confirmed as eternal as the solaric covenant, *"Thus saith the Lord; if my covenant be not with day and night, and if I have not appointed the ordinances of heaven and earth; then will I cast away the seed of Jacob, and David my servant, so that I will not take any of his seed to be rulers over the seed of Abraham, Isaac, and Jacob: for I will cause their captivity to return, and have mercy of them,"* (Jer 33:25-26, also see Ge 8:22). Therefore, since the sun still shines and the solar system still exists, God has not changed his mind regarding Israel. Throughout Bible times and up to the current time, God has always rewarded those who treated the Holy Land and the house of Judah as a friend, and judged those who regarded Israel as common or did harm to the nation and people.

Edom (Ezekiel 25:12-14)

Edom took revenge and greatly offended the house of Judah. They avenged themselves! As a result, they received God's vengeance and were completely destroyed and made waste. God has the wisdom and ability to make all things right without man's help. Our response must be one of love and mercy, for does not love fulfill all the requirements for God's blessings? Vengeance always brings a negative response from God! To God alone belongs vengeance, recompense, and judgment (Dt 32:35; Ro 12:19; Heb 10:30, a good lesson for all to learn in this day!) Each believer serves God and walks with Him. He has promised to take care of His people when they commit their ways unto Him.

Philistia (Ezekiel 25:15-17)

The Philistines were judged for revenge which grew out of their old hate. As a result, God said he would show them His revenge and anger. This attitude is still wide spread in the world today and will result in God's anger being directed at many present day nations. To take out revenge and hate on Israel is tantamount to trying to take out revenge on God.

Tyre (Ezekiel 26:2)

Tyre spoke against Jerusalem and rejoiced to see the city destroyed because it would increase their wealth. This attitude made them an enemy of Israel and also an enemy of God. Tyre was a great city with perfect beauty (Eze 27:4), but God is no respecter of persons or nations, and seeds sown always produce like fruit. While their external appearance was one of great beauty, they allowed themselves to be destroyed by pride, envy, and greed. They were glad to profit at the expense of Israel and even rejoiced at the calamity of God's anointed. How many nations today rejoice to see Israel have problems? How many nations hope that some other nation or group will do the job they would like to do? No doubt destruction awaits at the door of those who seek evil for Israel or encourage others to work evil so they can rejoice!

Zidon (Ezekiel 28:20-24)

Zidon was one among various other nations around Israel that treated God's people with despite. This is clearly an attitude God did not tolerate in that day nor will He tolerate an attitude of despite towards the things of God in this day.

These nations were likened to briers and thorns to the nation of Israel. Eventually briers and thorns have to be removed, and God said that he would remove the nations that dealt with Israel in this manner. Gentile nations are to be a blessing and help to Israel.

Egypt (Ezekiel 29:1-21)

Israel had gone to Egypt and depended upon Egypt for help, but Egypt was no better than a weak staff made of straw, a staff that was easily broken and caused injury in the process. As a result, when Israel trusted in Egypt, they were betrayed.

The example of Egypt would appear to have special significance to the United States. In recent years (since becoming a nation in

1948), Israel has requested help from the United States and trusted in the United States as a friend. Over the years the United States has given generously in both financial and military aspects. As a result, the United States has been blessed in many ways, and is currently the most powerful and wealthy nation on the earth. This is a fulfillment of God's promises given throughout the Scriptures to those who bless His interests.

As a result of this unique relationship, the United States is in a special situation to receive God's abundant blessings for being a partner with Israel or, on the other hand, God's cursings for refusing to help. As the United States responds as a friend to Israel, the nation will also be a friend of God. Being a friend of God has many benefits as is demonstrated in the life of Abraham.

Believers in the United States need to always pray that the day will never come when the government of the United States betrays that trust to Israel and becomes an enemy of God in the process. Praying over this matter becomes increasingly important as the American society moves away from Godly ways, and fewer and fewer elected leaders understand scriptural principles. The dangers in this regard increases greatly as Americans place less and less value on moral character and vote more to satisfy selfish desires in national elections. Also, America's financial dependence on world markets places more pressure on leadership to please world concerns. If the time ever comes when the United States rejects Israel or works against God's land, it will rapidly become a second-rate nation. A great danger exists today regarding various peace plans. The United States must never use its influence to push Israel into peace agreements that rebel against God's plan.

Some say the United States can no longer afford to stand behind Israel. Perhaps the question should be, can the United States afford not to bless Israel? Can the church afford not to bless Israel? We must ask, what is God's will and purpose in this matter? Obedience is the essence of blessings!

Israel is an eternal state in God's view and the land of Israel belongs to the house of Judah forever. Any nation coming against or speaking against Israel will be destroyed just as any nation being a blessing to Israel will be blessed. Throughout history, the fate of nations and leaders has been determined by their dealings with the house of Judah. Israel is a standard for the nations and Jerusalem is a balance in the hands of God. Nations and people chose to bless Israel and God or they chose to reject Israel and God. Understand, the Lord God of Israel is the one Lord God and His word is always absolutely correct.

Europe would be a very different place today if nations such as Spain, Germany, and Great Britain had responded as a trusted friend to the house of Judah during their time of glory and opportunity to bless. Missed opportunities often affect many generations.

Americans need to understand that the United States is in a dominate world position today in a large part because of its friendship with Israel over recent years. The most recent experience during the Gulf War illustrates the importance of this friendship. The Gulf War (1993) was won in the manner it was, as a result of the strong hand of God, not because of smart men or a great military force. This does not diminish the nature or strength of the United States military. But men need to understand that, before God, the military might of nations is not very important. In fact, it is counted as less than nothing and vanity, Isaiah 40:17, *"All nations before him are as nothing; and they are counted to him less than nothing, and vanity."* It is the Lord that gives strength (Isa 40:29-31).

The United States was blessed with a rapid victory with a very small loss of life because it was protecting Israel from an evil, rebellious nation and so, received God's special favor and blessing.

Babylon (Jeremiah 50:33-34)

Babylon was destroyed because it oppressed the people of Israel and would not let them go. God always hears the cry of the oppressed and will eventually set them free. In the process, destruction often comes to the oppressor. Jesus came to set free, and His people should be setting men free from spiritual as will as every other kind of oppression caused by men that follow Satan's ways.

Damacus/Syria (Isaiah 17:14)

Syria and Damacus were destroyed like any other nation (past or future) that plunders the Holy Land. Would men steal from God and expect to enjoy good things? Would men plunder what God has chosen as holy and expect him to turn and look the other way? Only a nation and people totally deceived and with out wisdom would be so foolish.

The Scriptures give us clear and important insights into what God requires of nations and people regarding their dealings with the Holy Land of Israel and the people of the house of Judah. The nations and people of the earth are totally without excuse if they chose to disobey God's instructions regarding His land and people. As the Scriptures say in Proverbs 8:1-3, "Wisdom crieth", but the question remains, who will hear? Will men listen?

The chart on the next page summarizes God's judgment on gentile nations regarding Israel. As these attitudes and actions bring God's judgment the reverse will bring God's blessings. They reveal to us how God expects nations and people to deal with His chosen people and nation. God has spoken, as always, the choice is up to men and nations.

"I have set before you life and death, blessing and cursing: therefore choose life" (Dt 30:19).

Nation & People Noted	Reason for God's Judgement *Actions of Enemies*	Reasons for God's Blessings *Actions of friendship*
Ammonites	Rejoiced at Israel's harm & despised the land	Prayer, concern and helping hand
Moab	Lack of respect, and called Israel common	Honor and gratitude
Edom	Revenge	Forgiveness
Philistia	Hate	Love
Tyre	Personal gain at the expense of others	Giving and generosity
Egypt	False trust, and betrayed Israel	Trusted and true friendship
Zidon	Scorn, briers, and thorns to the land of Israel	Serving, helping and peacemaker
Babylon	Oppressed and confined the house of Judah	Kindness, mercy & freedom
Damacus/ Syria	Spoil & rob	Build & strengthen

I believe the Scriptures teach us that the following attitudes and actions towards Israel are pleasing to God and will result in blessings to both Israel and the nations and people involved.

Concern	Love	Mercy
Intercession	Giving	Kindness
Honor	Friendship	Freedom
Gratitude	Peacemaker	Strengthen
Forgiveness	Serving	Building Up

The people of Israel have been scattered throughout the nations of the earth for many years, but in 1948 a small seed began to germinate. Over recent years that seed has received God's blessing and protection. As a result Israel has developed into a young tree. The tree has grown and is now spreading its branches over the land. Currently, buds and flowers are filling the tree, a sure sign that the fruit is in the development stages. As the fruit develops and grows, is not the "generation of harvest" upon us?

As the branches have developed and spread over the land, they have provided sites for *"the birds of the air"* (Mt 13:32) to lodge in the branches. This mixture of good and evil will cause conflict in the short term, but in the longer term, Christ will rule from Jerusalem. It is time to rejoice and be a part of God's plan for Jerusalem!

A City with Eternal Blessings

Arise to thy King, O Jerusalem.
Thy enemies run to and fro.
Thou shall be established forever.

Thy enemies profaned thy holy temple.
But the Lord of hosts destroyed their house.
Thou shall stand as a strong fortress forever.
Thy enemies called thee common and unclean.

But the Lord called for their judgment from heaven.
Thou shall be exalted far above them all for an inheritance.

Thy enemies took revenge on thee.
But the Lord's vengeance destroyed them without notice.
Thou shall find everlasting favor from the most high.

Thy enemies hate thee, O city.
But the Lord's anger made them as nothing.
Thou shall find everlasting love.

Thy enemies rejoiced at thy judgment.
But the Lord fed them pride and destruction.
Thou shall rejoice at thy eternal beauty.

Thy enemies called thee dead.
But the Lord hath given you new life.
Thou shall have abundant life forever.

Thy enemies despised thee.
But the Lord was their enemy.
Thou has an everlasting Friend.

Thy enemies betrayed thee.
But the Lord broke their staff.
Thou shall find a strong rod.

Thy enemies oppressed thee.
But the Lord made plunder of them.
Thou shall rejoice in eternal blessings.

Bless thy God always.
Favor and grace shall be yours.
Thou shall arise forever, O Jerusalem.

Chapter 7

A Window of Opportunity

"For as ye in times past have not believed God,
yet have now obtained mercy through their unbelief:
Even so have these also now not believed,
that through your mercy they also may obtain mercy.
For God hath concluded them all in unbelief,
that he might have mercy upon all."
—Romans 11:30-32

The true church, the body of Christ, is of one mind with God through Jesus Christ. Therefore, for the true body of believers the relationship with the land and people of Israel becomes a channel for demonstrating their love and commitment to God. Loving Israel in both word and deed becomes a part of loving God with body, soul, and mind. Remember, Jesus was born and lived in Israel as a Jew. He also selected Jewish disciples to start the early church. He also selected Paul, a Jewish Apostle to take the Gospel to the gentiles.

Believers should be in the forefront of blessing Israel and zealously promoting the kinds of attitudes and actions that bless God's special land and people. The gentile church should be eagerly taking the opportunity to fill the land of Israel with a multitude of blessings such as genuine concern for its well being, intercession with prayer and fasting, honor, gratitude, forgiveness, love, giving of material support, friendship, serving, mercy, kindness, strengthening and building. The Christian church should be overcoming every evil against the land by confronting it with good through the power of the Holy Spirit. God's mercy has great power to overcome evil.

The Christian church throughout the gentile nations must be at the forefront of blessing the newly developing church of believers in the Holy Land. The church in North America and Europe can no longer sit at ease with its rich staffs and large temple icons and not be concerned about the struggling church in the Holy Land. The early church in the gentile countries was eager to bless the believers in Jerusalem, and Paul commended them for this eagerness to bless (2 Cor 8:1-7).

The church (believers) is God's temple on earth (His house) and wealthy believers in the gentile nations must be concerned about God's house in the Holy Land. The warnings in Scripture is clear (see Haggai). If the established church in America does not change its ways, the church and the gentile nations will be judged. Now is the time to bless the Holy Land and raise a standard against the evil powers in the land.

The Bible's concept of love has powerful implications regarding the treatment of Israel and Jerusalem by believers. I believe God's blessings are increasingly going to depend on believers fulfilling the relationship of genuine love to Israel (1 Co 13, Ro 12; Jas 1:22-25). 1 John 3:18 says, *"My little children, let us not love in word, neither in tongue; but in deed and in truth."* To love in doctrine and by profession is not enough. We must demonstrate our love by definite acts; our love must be genuine. God is going to prove the church in this matter in the years ahead to see if we are genuine or simply speaking empty words.

Visitors

In God's view, believers have a broad range of responsibility in Israel. This includes the many believers that go to Israel as tourists each year. Having observed many tour groups in Israel, it seems that Christians who go to Israel as tourists must gain a new concept of their role. They need to view themselves as more than simple observers having a good time and blessing themselves, instead, become a part of what God is doing in the land.

Visitors to Israel must understand they are visiting more than ruins and historical sites. They are visiting a living, dynamic region in which God is rapidly bringing His plan together. The things that are taking place in Israel today are much more exciting than historical markers and events that took place thousands of years ago. It is important for believers to look ahead and see the heavenly Jerusalem in faith. Jerusalem is an eternal habitation of God's kingdom. Believers need to look at Jerusalem as God looks at the city. Since God is alive and working today, Jerusalem and the Holy Land have a future far greater than the past. Visitors to Jerusalem are visiting the City of God, the city of the great King and a land that is holy, a land that has a dynamic, eternal future!

Years ago, God destroyed all the abominations in the land that He declared holy, just as He destroyed the temple in Jerusalem. God wanted to give men full opportunity to let go of the past and follow Christ alone. But just as the old Jewish religious leaders rejected the "new thing" God was doing in Jesus, men today reject Jesus and keep digging up the "old things". Men continue to worship the "old things", going back to the "old ways", because they like religious traditions more than the ways of God. Most of the holy places that tourists visit in Israel are filled with nothing but religious traditions and idol worship. Over the places where Christ walked with fresh power and anointing, religious institutions have built icons to worship men and devils. People continue to study, rebuild, and worship at the pagan centers of Baal worship and considers them more interesting than the kingdom of God. As they do this, these old abominations are released to roam the land.

Men come to the Holy Land to honor the past and they forget that God wants obedience not sacrifice and that the "just shall live by faith". Which Jerusalem do we seek, the one of bondage or the one that is free (Gal 4:25-26)?

Jerusalem and Israel require respect, honor and the rewards of a great kingdom. When the Queen of Sheba came to visit King Solomon, she showed great respect for his kingdom and gave Solomon and his kingdom many gifts (2 Ch 9:1-12). As a result, the queen received all her desires and whatsoever she asked (2 Ch 9:12). Is not the same principle valid today? When we visit Jerusalem, we are visiting the city of a king far greater than Solomon and a kingdom with far greater wisdom and glory than the kingdom of Solomon.

Those who visit Jerusalem should be bringing blessing to the land, both in the spiritual realm and in the material realm. God will bless those who have an ear to hear and understand this principle. *"And she gave the King an hundred and twenty talents of gold, and of spices great abundance, and precious stones: neither was there any such spice as the queen of Sheba gave to King Solomon"* (2 Ch 9:9).

An Opportunity

In the future, when Jesus rules from Jerusalem, nations will be required to pay respect in Jerusalem (Rev 21:24). Today, we have the opportunity to bless the city and the land, not from fear of the law, but because of our love for Jesus and to be a part of the things He loves. Blessings will follow those who bless Israel. In our churches we sing praise to a Jewish Christ, should we also not love things and persons that He loves? Can we claim to love God and not care about the things that are close to His heart?

If we love God and abide in Him we will also love the things He loves. Scriptures are clear that God loves the land of Israel and the Jewish people. Deuteronomy chapter 28 provides a clear picture of

God's blessings and His curses as they relate to obedience. God may punish Israel (or any nation) for their rebellion according to His word, but His love and mercy remain forever the same. Israel will never be cast away or forgotten (Jer 51:5 and Ro 11). Our obedience always requires a response of love and mercy towards that which God loves. Loving Israel is at the minimum a matter of obedience for believers. As followers of Jesus move beyond obedience through obligation into genuine love, a multitude of blessings will flow out of the relationship.

God's desire is always towards Israel (Dt 32:10). He will not hold his peace or rest until His will for Zion and Jerusalem is completed (Isa 62:1).

I believe there is a warning in Amos that applies to the church today and particularly to the church in America, because American believers live in greater abundance than most other nations. Amos 6:1-6, *"Woe to them that are at ease in Zion, and trust in the mountains of Samaria, which are named chief of the nations, to whom the house of Israel came!"* The chapter goes on in verse six, *"but they are not grieved for the affliction of Joseph."*

This verse addressed the nation of Israel, but it is also a warning to the spiritual Zion, the church, and to all those who trust in men and enjoy riches not caring for the concerns of God who gave the riches. The Christian church in America is rich beyond measure, as described in verses 4, 5, and 6 and yet most of the church is not grieved for Israel. Spiritual Zion for the most part is more concerned with itself than with Israel (or God) and that is not pleasing to the Lord God of Israel.

The prophet Haggai 1:1-11 gives us timely insights into how God views and deals with men's actions that promote self interest over the interest of God. Jesus expressed this same concern in John 6:33.

In Haggai 1:11, the prophet rebukes the people of His day for living in ceiled houses and allowing the Lord's house to lie in waste. Because of this selfish attitude, a curse rested upon the people that resulted in the blessings of heaven and the fruits of the earth being stayed from them. Only after the people obeyed and feared the Lord did the Spirit of the Lord move over them to do the Lord's work. Once they walked in obedience, the Lord's blessings returned, even from that very day (Haggai 2:19).

The book of Haggai contains important principles that need to be understood by believers in this current age because Israel is again a nation being blessed by God. Today, the gentile nations as well as the wealthy churches in America have a similar self love, and are therefore in a similar situation.

The Lord of Israel has called for a drought, and the dews (blessings) from heaven along with the fruits of the earth are stayed due to lack of obedience. Christians of Western nations are living in ceiled estates, complacent and largely unconcerned about the Holy Land. At the same time, most Christian people are building kingdoms of wood, hay and stubble. There is going to be great loss when God's fire manifests the true nature of these houses (temples) (1 Co 3:12-15).

Until the church obeys and begins to fear God, the situation will continue to decline across the gentile lands. The only solution is obedience and a returning of believers to their first love, putting the things of Christ first and self far behind.

Currently, great importance must be attached to the Jewish people, the nation of Israel, the Holy Land and Jerusalem. All nations and especially the Christian gentile nations have a responsibility in these days to bless Israel both spiritually and materially after the manner of Cyrus. Certainly the church is without excuse because the church is told to be led by the Holy Spirit.

God has planned that the regathering of the nation of Israel and the building of Jerusalem should be a partnership between Jews and gentiles (Isa 60). Perhaps it is through this partnership that God will reveal himself anew to the Jewish nation.

From the very day the work is started, the Lord's blessings will return (Hag 2:18). Believers in America and other gentile nations have extravagant church buildings, most new believer groups in Israel have none. Believers in America have many rich pastors, the

Holy Land has only a few, most of whom struggle in the context of a persecuted church. When will the work of God take first place?

The Holy Land is currently in a struggle between Moslem and Jewish religions. Within both communities a Christian church exists that needs support (both spiritual and material) from the outside due to the extreme persecution both societies place on those who follow Christ. God has opened many doors for the gospel throughout the Holy Land in the last few years. The church in the gentile nations need to take more interest in and do more to support the Holy Land church in both the spiritual and material realms.

Christ's church needs to be grieving for Israel with prayer and fasting while giving material blessings (Am 6:6) for the new church in Israel as well as the nation. It is time for the church in America to reconsider its priorities (Ps 122:6-9).

Believers must ask themselves if it is pleasing to God for the church to pour massive sums of money into self-indulgent monuments and programs, while the new church in Israel is struggling for basic needs in many regions? The disciples remarked to Jesus about the temple in Jerusalem and he said that it would be gone shortly. Does the same hold true for our great temples of self-indulgent worship in North America? Are we also living at the end of an age when the icons of this period will not be carried over to the next?

The parable of the good Samaritan (Lk 10) has a lesson for believers regarding Israel at this point in time. The nation of Israel in the world today is much like the man among thieves. At every opportunity there are those who would try to strip the land, wound the people and leave the nation for dead (Lk 10:30). It must be the true believers in Jesus who have compassion and love for the land of Israel. Believers in recent years have been used by God to help Israel and they will continue to be used in this way. This has often been done through influence on governments of Christian nations like America. However, this is going to become more and more difficult as governments of formerly Christian nations become more and more deceived as their populations drift away from God's ways and have less understanding of scriptural principles.

I believe God has given very important aspects of the responsibility to restore Israel in these last days to the believing body of Christ (Ro 11:26, 31; Isa 61:6 and etc.). Certainly the role of peacemaker (Ps 122:6-9) falls squarely on the church because Jesus is the only source of real peace. Clearly, the responsibility of helping the developing church in the region rests on believers in the wealthy nations. Wealth is not given for self-indulgence but for the purposes of the kingdom of God. God will provide the resources if the church will waken to the commission and become involved in the great things God is doing in our day as he makes straight the way for the return of Jesus to earth.

As the new body of believers continues to grow and prosper in Israel, believers in the gentile nations must work with them to complete God's pleasure in building Jerusalem and laying the foundation for the temple. What God has started in Israel, He will continue to bless until it grows into one of the greatest demonstrations of God's glory ever manifested on the earth. What God has sown in Israel during this generation will mature into the church that will receive Christ when He returns to Jerusalem with the heavenly host!

God is seeking those who will read the vision and run with it (Hab 2:2-3). God wants people who will get involved in His programs. One of the most exciting things to occur in the history of man is taking place right now! Every believer in Jesus is called to be a part of what God is doing in Israel! The response of the church towards Israel must be one of prayer, love, rejoicing, and mercy! It is time to celebrate God's blessings and rejoice with Jerusalem!

Arise, Queen of Cities

Arise, Jerusalem, Queen of the earth.
You have found favor, holy Israel
Come for an anointing of oils and sweet odors.

Your king awaits you, Queen of the glorious land.
Come into His royal court.
Grace and favor await at your doorstep.

You have great blessings, Queen of holiness.
The invitations are sent, the feast is prepared.
The royal gifts are wrapped in fine white linen.

Put on your royal apparel, Queen of the earth.
The king sits upon His royal throne.
The golden sceptre is in his hand.

Stand in the inner court, Queen of glory.
The golden sceptre is given to you.
Come near and touch your salvation.

Make known your request, Queen of riches.
Favor is yours forever and ever.
All the kingdoms of the earth await you.

Your every petition is granted, Queen of Queens.
Power and glory is yours forever.
The King delights in you, Queen of His heart.

Blessed To Be A Blessing

God often uses those whom he has blessed to bless others. This principle also applies to Israel and the church, both in the realms of spiritual as well as material blessings. It is God's plan for those who have been blessed and received salvation through Israel (salvation came through Israel) to return the blessing on the nation and people of Israel in these last days (Ro 11:31-32), that Israel would also receive the fullness of God's mercy as promised. *"Even so have these also now not believed, that through your mercy they also may obtain mercy. For God hath concluded them all in unbelief, that he might have mercy upon all"* (Ro 11:31-32).

As was noted earlier, Israel is now a defined nation living in the promised land waiting for the fulfillment of God's promised blessings. Throughout history, Israel has received great material blessings from God (Dt 28) when its people obeyed Him. Through Jesus Christ, Israel gave the gentile peoples the fullness of spiritual blessings, the kingdom of heaven. Now, as we approach the end of this gentile age Israel is going to receive the fullness of spiritual blessing, as well as a great material blessing, as God releases His immense mercy upon the promised land through His nation of believers (spiritual nation).

Christ will reveal Himself to the Jewish people as the Holy Spirit works through His believers just as He revealed Himself to the gentiles through Holy Spirit-filled Jews in the book of Acts. As this happens, the latter rains will fall upon the promised land to produce a full and abundant harvest so that all the house of Israel may believe. However, it will be by the Holy Spirit of God and not the ways of men (Zec 4:6). As a result, only those led and anointed by the Holy Spirit can fully participate.

Many people have talked about an immense outpouring of the Holy Spirit to come upon the earth in the last days just prior to Christ's return. Will not the preponderance of this be the Holy Spirit outpouring on Jerusalem and the holy land? What other event could cause the latter rains to fall with such great intensity on a dry and parched land. The final outpouring upon Jerusalem to complete the great harvest will foreshadow the coming together of heaven and earth and also all people becoming one, no Jew or gentile in Christ (Eph 2:13-122) which Paul reveals will take place.

The outpouring of the Holy Spirit prophesied by Joel (2:28-29) came first to Jerusalem and I believe the Holy Spirit will complete the harvest from Jerusalem. Jerusalem has throughout history been the center of God's workings and that has not changed except for the period of years while Israel was scattered among the nations. However, Israel is again a nation in the promised land. Therefore, Jerusalem is again becoming the focus of what God is doing on the earth and a focal point of heavenly activity.

As in the past, major spiritual events will increasingly be centered in Jerusalem. As Jerusalem becomes the center of earthly and heavenly activity the transition of spiritual authority will be orderly and progressive but the trend from gentile nations to Jerusalem is irreversible. In the time ahead Israel will again be the center of spiritual activity as well as spiritual warfare until Jerusalem under the rule of Christ is the seat of worldwide spiritual authority.

Spiritual authority remained in the gentile nations only as long as Jerusalem was trodden down by the gentiles and the house of Israel was scattered throughout the nations. During that time spiritual authority remained in the gentile nations through believers filled with the Holy Spirit.

As the house of Israel is grafted back into the vine, it will gain preeminence, Romans 11:24, as God brings glory to His name through Israel. Our response as servants of God should be great rejoicing and prayer as we see the fulfillment of God's plan coming to completion. God has designed for believers to have an active part in this process.

Doing God's Pleasure a Second Time (Isaiah 11:11)

"Again the second time" the Lord shall regather His people from the four corners of the earth. We are living during that second time. It is taking place now! God is currently doing a very special thing in the earth; a thing very close to His heart. God is again working His pleasure on the earth through Israel and toward Israel. It is a glorious time in which we live! We are a chosen generation, but that

also brings responsibility!

In Isaiah chapters 44 and 45 we see God's pleasure expressed in five desires:

1. To raise a shepherd for His people (44:28; 45:13)
2. To rebuild Jerusalem (44:28)
3. To rebuild the temple (44:28)
4. To punish those nations that take His people captive (Jer 25:11-12)
5. To prove to Israel and the heathen nations that He is God (44:3-6)

God's pleasure is associated with the land of Israel and the house of Judah. If believers want to be participants in God's program they must desire and seek the things that He wants and work to complete His pleasure. As Jesus demonstrated, this is one of the keys to unity and friendship with God. God is making it increasingly plain to the entire world that His desire is with His people and He will accomplish that desire with great power and glory. Nations, people and believers will be proved and judged in part according to their response to God's desire regarding Israel and His people in the Holy Land.

As God works His pleasure a second time, I believe we can learn from the examples given to us in Scriptures from the first time God accomplished His pleasure regarding bringing His people home. This event is recorded in Isaiah chapters 44 and 45. This record in Isaiah and related Scriptures is a model which helps us understand how God may work to accomplish His pleasure today and how the end time believers of Jesus Christ may fit into the picture. Believers have more than just a passive role; they have a responsibility out of both debt and obedience. Every person alive has a debt to Israel and every believer must also be obedient to the voice of God.

8

GOD'S REVELATION REQUIRES A RESPONSE

"That saith of Cyrus, He is my shepherd,
and shall perform all my pleasures:
even saying to Jerusalem, Thou shalt be built;
and to the temple, the foundation shall be laid."
—Isaiah 44:28

Cyrus Anointed by God

Cyrus was anointed for the unique task of the first regathering of God's people so that Jerusalem would be rebuilt and that the temple foundation would be laid (Isa 44:28). In order to complete this task, God gave Cyrus incredible power and wealth. Resources from all parts of the world were channeled towards Jerusalem as a result. This was certainly a foreshadowing of the King that was coming to Jerusalem (Jesus) and also of what God would do in the end times as he prepared to establish His throne in Jerusalem.

Jerusalem was God's great pleasure at that time and Cyrus was given power over all the nations of the earth to complete the task

(Isa 45:1). Again today, we live in a unique time period when God is doing His pleasure in the land of Israel in preparation for major events. Believers are anointed to be partners in accomplishing God's great pleasure again toward the land of Israel as God gathers His people home for a second time, the final time. As a result, believers today are given equal or greater authority, power, and resources to complete this second regathering.

As we look at God's anointing of Cyrus for the first regathering of the Jews to Israel, I believe we see important parallels to the anointing of gentile believers for their part in the current (second) regathering. The anointing and actions of Cyrus help us understand how God views the responsibility of His people today. Are not we as believers in Jesus, who call ourselves the church anointed to carry out God's pleasure on the earth? What higher calling could we as individual believers and as a body have in today's world that God would choose us to help in this unique task that is so close to His heart? This is a great honor as well as a responsibility that we must respond to with all our might and strength. Would we dare ignore our King's prime pleasure? Our first desire must be His total pleasure (Mt 6:33 and Rev 2:4-5)! This is the day of joy, celebration, and comfort – not a time to cry and mourn.

If God will not rest or be at peace until His desire for Jerusalem is fulfilled (Isa 62:1), how can we as His servants rest until God's prime desire is fulfilled? This is especially true at such a time as this when we see all the things coming together for the great day of the Lord. Is there not a joy and anticipation to the times? Is not this a day to rejoice and watch?

In Isaiah 44:28, God said that Cyrus was a shepherd to His people. In those days, God often raised up men who received the anointing of the Holy Spirit for a specific task as did Cyrus (Isa 44:28 and 45:13). Today, God has given His anointing to believers in fullness through the Holy Spirit to do all of His pleasure. Cyrus had a couple of important and very interesting historical characteristics in his background that we see paralleled in the church.

One, he came from a mixed marriage of a gentile father and a Jewish mother. Both were equal partners (Est 5:6). As a result Jews and gentiles shared fully in the event. The church is also a mixture of the two parts, so today, both are to be fully involved in the regathering and rebuilding process. Both are involved, but each branch of the vine has its own role as the Holy Spirit directs.

Two, Cyrus was ruler of a mighty gentile nation that was given enormous power by God in order to perform His pleasure regarding the Jews and Jerusalem. The church is also a nation (God's holy nation) centered in the great wealthy gentile political powers of our day for the purpose of being a shepherd over Israel. God has chosen to use the Christian gentile nations of the world to protect His land and people during the establishment period, so that Israel would grow into a strong tree with good fruit. As this process comes to maturity the harvest will be a nation that will witness to the world of God's power and glory.

Without God's protective hand, Israel would have been destroyed by its enemies several times (Ps 124). The church (like Cyrus) is world wide (all nations) and in the spiritual realm has authority over great political and material power and wealth. This has been God's plan to protect His people during this period (the second regathering) and must continue as God fulfills His purpose through the Holy Land.

Cyrus was given the anointing of God just as the church is given the anointing of God today for the purpose of doing God's pleasure in the Holy Land. The revival of the Christian church in the late eighteen hundreds and early nineteen hundreds, after many years of darkness, was ordained by God so that Israel would be reestablished as a nation. The rise of wealth and power in the free world nations of the West was again ordained by God for the establishment and protection of Israel. More recently the wealth and increasing power of "emerging nations" throughout the earth is ordained by God for the blessing of Israel and for God's divine purpose to produce fruit in the land. The gentile nations of the earth must become wealthy so that this wealth can be converted to Israel in God's time (Isa

60:5). The church of Jesus has been a major player in all these events and will continue to participate until God's plan for Israel is mature.

In the first gathering, a man and a specific nation was chosen because the gathering was for a physical purpose, to raise up a material nation. However, this time, while the regathering also has a physical aspect, its spiritual aspect is more important. Therefore, this time God will use a spiritual power (the church) to manifest His presence that Israel as a nation will receive the kingdom of God and know her true King, thus, believers are taking the role of Cyrus.

Shepherd
Cyrus: a pattern for building and laying a foundation in Israel.

Cyrus was anointed a shepherd to Israel (Isa 44:28). He was a protector and guide in the regathering. However, the church in this time of history has been and is expected to continue fulfilling a similar role as protector and shepherd of the nation of Israel. Believers must be willing to defend the nation in a very practical way as a shepherd would do in time of danger, but foremost believers must be spiritual protectors through prayer and intercession. Through prayer and fasting believers have total authority on this earth to work God's pleasure (Mt 16:19 and 21:21-22). This includes authority over all nations and the wealth of the earth.

Perform All My Pleasure

Cyrus achieved the pleasure of God without a full understanding (Isa 45:4-5), believers often walk in faith, also without a full understanding (faith does not require understanding). However, we must understand that the church is taught by the Holy Spirit (Jn 16). Therefore, believers must be seeking God with prayer and fasting for His will and pleasure regarding Israel and the new church that is taking shape in the Holy Land. Once His pleasure is revealed to us then we must be obedient to execute His pleasure with all out body, soul, and mind that we may prosper in all His works as did Hezekiah (2 Ch 31:21). We can be assured that as we are led and anointed by the Holy Spirit He will perform God's pleasure through us (Jn 16:13-15).

Proclaiming the Restoration of Jerusalem

As a result of God's anointing, Cyrus ruled over a great empire. Therefore, he had the political and military power as well as the wealth to proclaim the restoration of Jerusalem and it would be done.

Believers today are anointed by the same God who has all power and authority in heaven and earth! In Jesus Christ by the power of the Holy Spirit, they can also proclaim God's pleasure and expect the authority and anointing to see it done (Eph 1:19-23). The political and military power of nations are as nothing to God (Isa 40:17). Believers are given the power to bind and loose on earth (Mt 16:19). Believers need not fear the embassies of Satan that inhabit the land around Israel (2 Ch 32:7-8). They have always been present and will be until Jesus returns with the army of heaven to destroy them. These enemies of God have no more authority over God's anointed today than did Pilate over Jesus. *"Thou couldest have no power at all against me, except it were given thee from above"* (Jn 19:10-11).

By prayer, fasting and works of mercy those who believe what God has said will, proclaim Jerusalem and the Holy Land restored by the power of God and see it accomplished with great wonder. Jesus is coming with the armies of heaven to claim His land and rule the earth in righteousness. Believers are on this earth to help prepare the way!

Jerusalem Restored

Arise, O Jerusalem; Arise, O eternal city.
Arise, in fresh splendor and eternal glory.
Arise, to receive the glory of your King.

May peace flow to you like a great, still river.
May prosperity flow through all your gates.
May God's Holy Spirit flow from your sanctuary.

Come, to great peace like a never ending river.
Come, to great prosperity like a great flood.
Come, to meet your mighty eternal King of Kings.

Foundation of the Temple

Cyrus laid the foundation for the temple in his day according to God's instructions. Believers are also called to lay the foundation of a temple, the temple of Jesus! I suspect the principle function of the present day church is to labor in partnership with the Holy Spirit to lay the foundation of a spiritual temple in Israel. This day, believers are a part of a spiritual kingdom, the kingdom of Heaven, and represent the temple of God as the Holy Spirit abides within them. Eventually all who live in Jerusalem will be filled with righteousness because all will be one in Christ. As believers (all one in Christ, both Jews and Gentiles) fill Jerusalem, the foundation of a spiritual temple will arise in the Holy City.

This is one of the major reasons it is important for believers to go to Israel and become involved. Jerusalem is God's holy city and we are a part of His kingdom. Believers must take spiritual authority over the city and work to prepare for the return of Jesus. Such activities as making friends, praying, and blessing the land are important. Also supporting the Christian church in the land with prayer and fasting as well as material help is important. Through these manifestations of love and mercy, God's people will have their eyes opened to Jesus the Messiah.

We are told in Romans 11:26 that all Israel will believe. Through prayer, fasting, and showing God's mercy to Israel, the foundation of the spiritual temple is now being laid in Jerusalem.

Anointed

Cyrus was anointed to do the pleasure of God (Isa 44:28). We as believers are also anointed to do the pleasure of God (2 Co 1:21; 1 Jn 2:27-28). For what other reason would God anoint His people? Jesus said that was the reason He came! What a prodigious opportunity to be chosen to participate in one of God's greatest desires. Good servants always do the pleasure of their master, but to be selected for such a high calling by the King is reason for great joy along with particular attention to obedience. God would desire that every detail be accomplished with perfection and His great glory be demonstrated.

As a result of the divine anointing on Cyrus, God performed a number of great works. Through the divine anointing on Cyrus, God so prepared the environment of the kingdom that Cyrus could not help but accomplish the work set before him. As believers in the same God, who never changes, it is important for us to understand that as we are anointed of God we also can not fail in doing His pleasure. God's anointing always comes with the environment and fullness to complete the task. It is by God's power that we accomplish His work, not our abilities. If we understand these truths of God's kingdom, we can never fail.

Six aspects of God's anointing on Cyrus continue to be given to believers today as they are obedient to do God's pleasure in the Holy Land.

First, Cyrus received immense power. He had power to subdue nations and change the political face of the earth. As believers in Jesus and temples of His Holy Spirit we have even greater power in the spiritual realm by prayer and fasting (2 Co 10; Eph 1:19-23). Just as no mountain could stand before Zerubbabel's anointing to finish the restoration of the temple (Zec 4:7), so no mountain whatsoever can stand before God's people this day, as they lay the foundation on what God is doing in Jerusalem at this time (Mt 21:21-22).

Second, Cyrus had doors opened for him. God still opens doors and will continue to open doors so that believers can do His pleasure regarding Israel. No door can remain shut that God wants open! Is not Zerubbabel made a signet (seal) as to what God will do in the final days (Hag 2:23).

Third, Cyrus was told that the Lord would go before him. The Lord also goes before us, but we must learn to follow Him step by step. God has prepared the way, He has given us His Holy Spirit to lead us in the prepared way, and He provides angels to protect and keep us along the path. The presence of God's Holy Spirit always goes with His anointing and His anointed. God's Holy Spirit will do the mighty works of power in the same way Zerubbabel experienced (Zec 4:6). The vision of the golden candlesticks and the two olive trees is also a word for God's people in our time as they work to restore Israel and Jerusalem (Zec 4:1-4). *"Not by might, nor by power, but by my spirit, saith the Lord of Hosts"* (Zec 4:6).

Fourth, Cyrus was told that the purpose of the Lord's going before him was to make crooked places straight. Currently, the crooked places are being made straight in preparation for Christ's return. As we learn to walk in God's anointing and power, walk through doors that are opened, and delight in His presence we will walk in straight places. As this happens, Israel will be saved, the Jerusalem church will grow in power and authority, and Christ will return.

Fifth, Cyrus was told that the gates of brass and bars of iron would be destroyed. The protective devices of men have no power to stop the anointing of God. The gates of obstacles will be destroyed and iron bars that hold the locks will be cut apart. Even the strongest defenses on earth have no ability to hold back the anointing of God. We as believers must understand how absolutely awesome the anointing of God is when we walk in obedience to His pleasure! This is particularly true where the restoration of Israel is involved because all power and authority is given to complete this desire of God. Remember, God can do anything and will do everything required to see that His every word is true.

Sixth, Cyrus was given the treasures of darkness and the hidden riches of secret places. Everything on this earth belongs to God, and He has all power and authority over all His creation. This includes all the riches of this present day evil world system. God has made it all available to work His works. As Cyrus performed the pleasure of God, he was given the greatest riches of the entire world that he would know who God was and that he would be able to complete the task (Isa 45:3). Presently, as believers do God's will regarding Israel, they will be instruments in God's hand to channel the riches of this world to carry out God's pleasure. In the years ahead, God will, take the wealth of the gentile nations and use it to bless His nation (Isa 60:16 and 66:11).

The Responsibility of Wealth

Since Cyrus was given great wealth from God, this aspect of his kingdom gives us interesting insights into the relationship of man, wealth and ministry.

It is important to understand the source, purpose and responsibility of wealth from God's point of view. While wealth is an instrument of God for His purpose (only one of many), many believers have been destroyed by Satan's deception regarding its use. The church presently has many erroneous ideas regarding money and wealth in the kingdom of God, because people have listened to the doctrines of men instead of the Holy Spirit. Man tends to orient things to benefit himself while the Holy Spirit always orients things directly toward the will of God. We must be shown by the Holy Spirit and understand wealth from God's view point, if we want to please him and accomplish His purposes with His resources.

The Kingdom View

First, wealth belongs to God and He is the one who gives it. Therefore, God channels His resources to who He wills for His reasons and purposes for His glory. He also gives instructions regarding its use and judges the use of that which He gives according to His standards.

Man has the idea that he earns wealth (Satan's deception), but that is a carnal understanding. In truth, wealth is given by God for His purposes. Earning wealth is a waste of time because it has no value (Isa 55:1-2 and Mt 6:25-34). What man receives from God is by grace through faith, all of our ways are unrighteousness before him that is righteous (Ro 3:10-18). Man has no way to earn anything from God! Wealth is a blessing of God's love that flows out of obedience to God's ways (Dt 28:1-14), one can not earn that which overtakes him (Dt 28:2). Abram understood this principle when he refused goods from the king of Sodom (Ge 14:23). The principle is again illustrated in 2 Ch 1:11-12 when Solomon asked for wisdom and was given riches and wealth as a favor because God loved him. Jesus related the same idea in Matthew 6:33, *"But seek ye first the kingdom of God, and his righteousness; and all these things shall be added unto you"*.

Second, true wealth must bring glory to God because it cannot be obtained from man. All wealth (little or much) is given by God, so the purpose of wealth is to bring glory to His name for this is the purpose of all that God does. Therefore, it should be the purpose of all that we do also because we are led by His Holy Spirit who always brings glory to Jesus.

We are told to ask God for that which we require, John 14:13-14, He alone is our source. To trust man for anything will bring curses from God (Jer 17:5). This concept is common throughout both the Old and New Testaments. A striking example is found in the life of Abraham (Ge 14:22-23), *"And Abram said to the king of Sodom, I have lift up mine hand unto the Lord, the most high God, the possessor of heaven and earth. That I will not take from a thread even to a shoelatchet, and that I will not take any thing that is thine, lest thou shouldest say, I have made Abram rich.* " No place in Scripture do we find true men of God asking other men for anything! Seek God and God alone!

Paul clearly understood the concept of wealth in the kingdom of God. That is why he chose not to use his authority in this manner and worked to support his ministry (1 Co 12:23 and Ac 20:33-35). He understood the importance of being free of obligation to man. He also implied that requesting gifts from man for himself was one step away from covetousness (Ac 20:33).

Wealth, like everything in heaven and earth, is God's resource. It is the job of the Holy Spirit to direct the distribution and use of wealth, for only the Holy Spirit knows the perfect will of God regarding the use of God's resources. Accordingly, only those led by the Holy Spirit can make the right choice. Every person is instructed to be led by the Holy Spirit. As a result, one man can not tell another person how to use this resource of God. For one person to tell another person how to use God's resources is to usurp authority from the Holy Spirit. Those who steal authority from the Holy Spirit will be held responsible. Believers must stop taking dominion and authority over the lives of other believers for their benefit (Mt 20:24-28 and Jn 21:22)!

Since wealth is given abundantly and freely by God for His purpose, why are ministries that claim to be God's anointed so often synonymous with begging, and harassment for money to do "God's purpose?" This behavior is not scriptural. God is not a beggar, a God that can build a city of pure gold and use precious stones in the foundations (Rev. 21:18-20) does not need anything from man. This same God has given authority in His kingdom and given all things in Christ therefore, we must ask Him! That which is received from God is blessed of God, but that which is received from men is blessed by men and of no value to God. If you want the kingdom of God then ask God! If you want the "kingdom of this earth," then ask men! We get what we seek!

"Cursed be the man that trusteth in man, and maketh flesh his arm, and whose heart departeth from the Lord" (Jer 17:5). Asking men for money is getting on dangerous ground. It borders on idolatry and is a sister to witchcraft. The practices of fund raising and requesting offerings in the name of Jesus is a tradition of religion and reflects man's way of doing his thing. This practice has its roots in paganism not the kingdom of God. Covetousness is a work of the flesh and brings death. Those who practice it shall not inherit the kingdom of God (1Co 5:10-11, and Eph 5:5); covetous practices are a sign of the last days (2 Ti 3:2); and a sign of apostasy (2 Pe 2:14). Covetousness opens the door to every problem.

The Scriptures teach it is acceptable to take money for the work of the gospel (1Co 9:9-11), but Paul also reveals that there is a better way. Do we choose God's best or the ways of others? The wide way has many pit falls and dangers as we see all around us today. Can not God provide?

Third, wealth is given for the purpose of building God's kingdom. Believers have been given wealth to do the work of the Lord. Wealth accumulated simply for the purpose of blessing one's self brings death (Lk 12:16-21).

Blessing Israel is an important part of God's plan today and believers need to be using their wealth to bless the land and the church in the Holy Land. This is one way to bless God. As with Cyrus, this must not be for reward (Isa. 45:13). If you want to get rich or receive personal gain from the Lord's work, then find another ministry. God has required that this labor to the Holy Land must be a task of obligation, mercy, and love without price or reward. Jesus, the disciples, Paul and others gave everything that the gentiles might believe and receive the kingdom of God. We must have the same kind of commitment, that Israel might believe. Personal desires must be put aside. Believers are already in debt to Israel and the Jewish people. Now is the time to set free without price or reward.

A Scriptural Model for Mercy and Blessings

"Thus saith Cyrus king of Persia, The Lord God of heaven hath given me all the kingdoms of the earth; and he hath charged me to build him an house at Jerusalem, which is in Judah.

Who is there among you of all his people? his God be with him, and let him go up to Jerusalem, which is in Judah, and build the house of the Lord God of Israel, (he is the God,) which is in Jerusalem.

And whosoever remaineth in any place where he sojourneth, let the men of his place help him with silver, and with gold, and with goods, and with beasts, beside the freewill offering for the house of God that is in Jerusalem" (Ezra 1:2-4).

This Old Testament proclamation provides a model for believers who want to become involved in doing God's pleasure in Israel today.

First, the proclamation set all Jews free to go to Jerusalem. The Lord has proclaimed freedom for all Jews to return to Israel again in this generation and it is now taking place. God ordained that the gentiles would have an important part in this process (Isa 60:9, 66:20).

Second, the proclamation provided that they go in blessings. To accomplish this objective, the proclamation provided that neighbors would give the Jewish travelers silver, gold, goods, and beasts for their personal needs. (This is similar to what God did when the people left Egypt, Exodus 11:2 and 12:36). Free will offerings were also to be given for the temple. Beyond this, Cyrus also gave them good wishes and such things as they needed from supplies out of his kingdom. In the second (current) regathering, the gentiles also have a similar mandate (Isa 60:9-10).

As a result of this proclamation, not only did the people from all parts of the kingdom contribute to bless Israel, but all nations under the authority of Cyrus (all the kingdoms of the earth, Ezra 1:2) contributed to bless Israel. This is also in accord with God's plan today. People throughout the whole earth are expected to help the Jewish people become established in Israel and rebuild the nation.

All nations of the earth are expected to (and will be required to) contribute from their resources (Isa 60:1-22; 61:6 and 66:20). Contributions are required for both the general and personal needs of the people as well as the needs for building a (spiritual) temple (believers must play a special role here).

Under God's plan proclaimed by Cyrus, seed money from various sources was given to the Jewish people for the project and they were responsible to get at the work and complete the task. They become established in the land and then obtained materials and went to work doing as they were instructed by God. God sent them into the land with blessings.

I believe the first regathering under Cyrus was a pattern for this current time, which the Lord is using and will continue to use the same concept. Believers in the West, particularly the wealthy nations, have a special role to play in the process. God had given these gentile nations great wealth that His name be glorified. Israel is the ultimate instrument to bring glory to God's name throughout the whole earth. Accordingly, God requires that this wealth be returned to His land and people (Isa. 60:5).

Current events must reflect this pattern as a foreshadowing of the future kingdom. As people become involved in blessing Israel according to God's purpose and walk by His Spirit, they will become a channel for a great outpouring of God's glory. God's glory that flows into and out of Israel in these last days will be like nothing ever experienced before on the earth. Those in the channel of that great river will receive a blessing and anointing not previously known to man as the latter rains fall to complete the harvest. However, it is clear that God will not anoint or allow His Holy Spirit to work through the ways of men. God clearly hates the ways of men and religious traditions (Jer. 17:5). They bring nothing but curses and problems. The Holy Spirit of God will anoint and flow through only that which is pure and holy as He brings glory to a holy God.

One way or another, God will direct the worlds resources toward Israel to complete His plan on the earth (Isa. 60). We can see this happening in various ways today as we read and watch the news events. Our blessing comes as we understand what God is doing and eagerly seek to be a part of what He is working on the earth.

Five Fold Prophecy

Isaiah 45:13 gives a five fold prophecy regarding Cyrus. This same five fold prophecy also applies to present day believers as they work God's pleasure in bringing about the restoration and regathering of Israel.

Instruction for present day believers:
1. Be raised up in righteousness
2. Be directed in His ways
3. Build a city
4. Let captives go
5. Do not do these things for reward

If present day believers are going to receive the same kind of anointing revealed in Isaiah 44 and 45, they must be committed to doing the pleasure of God out of love and obedience regardless of the cost. Paul understood that kind of commitment as he made the gospel available to the gentiles. Certainly such a glorious heavenly commission and promise requires no less!

A great opportunity is before those who believe and have an ear to hear what the Lord is saying in this time. Throughout all of history, only believers in this generation have this unique opportunity and commission. Many have looked for this time and wanted to be a part of it. However, we are blessed with the opportunity of this unique time in God's plan. What a tragedy to have lived during this time and passed it up or missed the opportunity. Believers must cast off the deadly complacency of our times and walk in the power of the Spirit of God. Those who abide in the anointing of God for this task will receive a glory and anointing unseen before in history. God is in the process of doing what the whole Bible talks about and the whole earth awaits. What a time in which we live! We can have a part in doing one of God's greatest pleasures!

Believers should be rejoicing and giving praise for what God is doing on the earth today. While the things of this world are slipping into confusion, God is bringing to completion prophetic words from all parts of the Scriptures. If our eyes are focused on this world, we will have despair and confusion, but if we are focused on heavenly events we will have great joy and praise as we wait in anticipation for our Lord to return.

Therefore let us be about the works of God:
1. Building the free Jerusalem
2. Laying the temple foundation
3. Opening the doors of God's mercy on Israel

Let us be about the work with a commitment that cannot fail:
> *"And in every work that he began in the service*
> *of the house of God, and in the law, and in the*
> *commandments, to seek his God, he did it*
> *with all his heart, and prospered" (2 Ch 31:21)*

Fulfilling God's Pleasure

God is anointing believers in this day to accomplish His great delight in Israel in at least two important ways. The first, is to accomplish the physical building of a nation and city through political and material support. Second, is the spiritual phase as the nation and people are set free to the truth regarding Jesus. These two events will come about in the fullness of time as God's people (believers) demonstrate God's pleasure in love and mercy to His chosen people and nation. The fulfillment of God's plan is a simple act of love and obedience. The key to demonstrating God's pleasure is mercy. Closely associated with the anointing to demonstrate God's mercy is a life of prayer and fasting for Israel and Jerusalem plus an ability to rejoice with the land and people. Scriptures admonish the friends of God to pray for peace, to love, to rejoice with, and to show mercy towards Jerusalem. Believers must give praise and rejoice at what is taking place in Jerusalem. God wants believers to be a part of the rejoicing and gladness so they will be a partaker of the comfort and blessings associated with the holy Jerusalem.

Rejoicing and Praise

Jerusalem, be filled with the people of praise.
Praising the Lord of hosts forever, everywhere over the land.
Streets, be filled with dancing and let praise fill the air.

Israel, sing forth the sacrifices of praises as a spring rain.
Praising the Lord throughout the land, like a mighty river.
Goodness and mercy come down as the eternal rains.

Jerusalem, the voices of joy shall flow forth from every gate.
Voices of joy shall be an honor to all nations of the earth.
For the Lord of hosts will inhabit your joy and praise.

Israel, the voice of gladness shall fill your cities.
The Lord's goodness shall bring fear to all nations.
Shall not the nations tremble at your great blessings?

Jerusalem, Israel, rejoice and arise in eternal splendor.
The Lord of Hosts has called forth His joy and praise.
Let the people of praise fill Jerusalem with every holy song.

Those anointed for this task will be blessed for the purpose of blessing Israel and its people. Surely, it is God's pleasure that Israel receive her blessing (Isa 66:9). For we are told that the Lord will not hold His peace or rest until righteousness and salvation fill Jerusalem (Isa 62:1).

God seeks to use the believers living in these last days to prepare the way for Israel to receive His desire of righteousness, peace, and blessings. Isaiah 61:3-11 describes the state of Israel after Christ comes and sets up His rule on the earth. God is now in the process of preparing Israel for this exalted time. He has chosen gentile believers to have a part in this restoration process (Isa 60, 61 and 66). In Christ, through the Holy Spirit, He has given His followers absolute power and authority to do His will on the earth.

Response of the Gentile Church

"Boast not against the branches" (Ro 11:18) and *"be not high minded, but fear"* (Ro 11:20). Our treatment and actions toward Israel reflects our understanding and love for God. If we are filled with God's love, we will also love that which God loves. Otherwise, we cannot be in unity with Him. God's love toward Israel is clear throughout Scriptures!

I believe the story of the good Samaritan gives us important understanding of our responsibility toward Israel and the developing church in the Holy Land.

The key word is **mercy**. The practical demonstration of mercy in an attitude of love becomes critical as we consider our response toward Israel and the house of Judah. This is communicated by Paul in Romans chapter 11, particularly verses 30-32. Verse 31 says, *"Even so have these also now not believed, that through your mercy they also may obtain mercy."*

I believe Paul is revealing that through mercy, gentile believers are going to have a part in bringing salvation to Israel and the Jews. We need to take note that it is through mercy, and not using the methods that we may think are good. It will take more than sermons and tracks to annul the effects of "religious" and "Christian" cruelty to the Jews throughout history. Believers need to forget about religious tradition, self-interest, man's methods, and sermons, and exhibit a genuine, Christ filled love that manifests the fullness of God's mercy. Only manifestations of genuine kindness and mercy can break down these walls of mistrust. No other method will work. If we are going to work the works of God we must walk in His anointing and be led and directed by the Holy Spirit in the ways God has chosen. It is *"not by might, nor by power, but by my spirit, saith the Lord of hosts"* (Zec 4:6). We must reveal God's glory in our lives, not any religious pretense of man's ways. Genuineness is possible only as the Holy Spirit lives within us.

Now is the time for believers to bless Israel with every kind of mercy and love that they might see the truth about Jesus. What a glorious finish to the gentile age! We should be humbled that God has given gentile believers this glorious opportunity. Let us listen, hear, and obey that we do not miss anything God is saying regarding Israel. Remember, God did not say through teaching or preaching, but through mercy. It is not the responsibility of gentile believers or gentile nations to preach to Israel or put demands on them. God's plan is for believers to simply put on Christ, and let His river of divine mercy and love flow through them. Only through obedience to the word of God will gentile believers have a part in this blessing to Israel.

Calling Forth, Arise Jerusalem

Jesus often spoke by command with absolute authority because He always spoke the will of the Father. The Father showed Him all things (Jn 5:20). We are encouraged to do the same thing because the Father has promised to show us all things also (Jn 16:13-15). Jesus spoke as ruler of a victorious kingdom to a defeated kingdom (Lk 11:16-23). Victorious kingdoms do not ask defeated kingdoms, they command with authority. True believers are ambassadors of that victorious kingdom of heaven on earth and therefore should act accordingly. God has given believers a diplomatic protocol from heaven and he expects His ambassadors to follow His program. Through the Holy Spirit, we should be in constant contact with our heavenly headquarters (1 Th 5:17). The Holy Spirit knows all that takes place in heaven and earth and is commissioned to show us all that God has given for us to know (Jn 15).

We are a part of the most advanced communications system in the world and need not lack in anything. However, we must keep our lines open to heaven so that we have a constant flow of information and instructions. Only God has a full perspective of the battlefield. We need constant input regarding the enemy and every situation. Through the Holy Spirit, we have a personal, twenty-four hour line directly to the throne of God in heaven.

We see an example of this in John 11:43 as Jesus called forth Lazarus. Jesus was able to speak with authority because He had been shown by the Father at some time prior to the event (Jn 11:4-6; 41). Jesus understood the situation, the timing of events and procedures to follow. As always, He was walking in perfect obedience and anointing of the Holy Spirit, under the full anointing of God's wisdom, understanding, counsel, might, knowledge, and the fear of the Lord (Isa 11:1). We also need this full anointing to do God's perfect will.

In this miracle, we also see another analogy to God's plan for the present day nation of Israel. Another aspect of the believer's role regarding Israel today is that of calling forth the resurrection of the nation and the city of Jerusalem to arise from death to glorious life. It is time for believers to call forth in prayer, in song and in psalms. Simply speaking the will of God can have great power over the kingdoms of darkness (see also Ezekiel chapters 34-37 regarding the power to call forth).

We see a five step process in the resurrection of Lazarus that is analogous to the church's role in the resurrection of Jerusalem in this time and season.

> **Step 1:** Prepare the way - This will take place through prayer, fasting and obedience to the word of God.
> **Step 2:** Remove the stone - Mercy is the power to remove the stone of blindness and let in the light of the Gospel. Once the stone is removed the light will overtake the darkness.

Step 3: Call forth to arise - As believers call forth to Jerusalem the city will arise to its destiny in Christ.
Step 4: Loose - The city will come forth bound but will be set free as the cords of the law are removed and the Gospel of Jesus fills the land.
Step 5: Let him go - Jerusalem will then walk in God's light under the power of the Holy Spirit.

We see another example of calling forth in Ezekiel chapters 34-37. The prophet is told to speak directly to nations, people and the land. For example, in chapter 36:4, Ezekiel is told to speak to the mountains, hills, rivers, valleys, and cities. In chapter 37, Ezekiel is told to speak regarding Israel. These Scriptures are examples for believers today. God also wants His people today to speak and prophecy to lands, situations, nations, and people that His will be completed. As God's people speak to Jerusalem the city will take on new life and be resurrected according to God's divine plan.

A NEW DAY

Awaken and arise, O Jerusalem.
Remove the sand from your eyes and look East.
Your glory cometh on the wings of the cherubim's.

You have slumbered through a long night.
Now the day breaks forth with brightness.
Arise and prepare for thy King, O City.

This is the day prophesied by your prophets.
They said this day would come.
The bride rejoices with you, arise!

Chapter 9

GOD REQUIRES MERCY

Samaritan:
A Practical Application and Response
(Luke 10:30-37)

The story of the good Samaritan has valuable practical applications as we seek to understand what God is saying to the church regarding the Holy Land. It is critical that believers respond to God's pleasure regarding the Holy Land in a very practical way. This pragmatic view point is especially important when dealing with the cultures of the region.

The parable of the good Samaritan is a story that illustrates a good, pragmatic, hands on demonstration of mercy (Lk 10:37). Therefore, it teaches us how God views mercy and what he expects from us in a down-to-earth way as we extend mercy to Israel and the Holy Land region.

Clearly, Israel as a nation and people have received all the harm that befell the man in the parable. The land and people have been stripped and wounded and left for dead by men of evil actions with no compassion.

Yet, even today, many pass by as did the priest who was only curious. The priest may well represent the religious establishments of this world today who pass by on the other side for many reasons. As they pass by for whatever reason, the man remains the same. Many Levites, or religious people, came and looked out of curiosity and self interest, but then pass by on the other side. Yet the state of the man remained the same. He was left to die without real concern or compassion.

However, in the parable is a third person, the Samaritan, who made a difference and changed the condition of the man. The Samaritan was humble and showed compassion. The Samaritan showed mercy and as a result changed the state of the man from death to life. God's mercy always brings life out of dead situations. This is what God wants from people today, those who will forget personal desires and show mercy to His nation and people so that Israel will also be changed from death to life. God had mercy on us, and through Christ He changed our state from death to life. Now it is our turn, we are called to do the same for His nation and people. The story of the Samaritan represents an example for believers who want to help fulfill God's pleasure toward Israel today in a practical way and make a difference.

The Manifestations of Mercy

Mercy is not in word only, but also in deed (James 1:22-25).

1. He bound up the wounds.

Binding up wounds is a form of protection both from additional infection and decay as well as from loss of life giving blood. Only as believers bind up wounds through God's love is there hope of life. The bandage of love and mercy will start the healing process! As each fresh bandage is applied, the healing progress is enhanced and new vigor is restored.

2. He poured in oil and wine.

Oil and wine bring peace and comfort and begins the healing process. Perhaps the oil represents the healing action while the wine is the purifying action. The two work together and allow the body to rebuild both mentally and spiritually. The oil and wine end the death process and allow the beginning of new life to take hold. Believers need to pour in the oil of anointing through prayer, and fasting, and through practical demonstration of mercy. As this is done the new wine of the gospel will flow over the land and its people. The oil and wine will bring gladness and joy to the land and the people.

3. He put him on his own beast.

Perhaps this illustrates the willingness of the Samaritan to give of himself and put his comfort and concerns aside to care for the wounded man. He was starting to invest more and more of himself in the well-being of the stranger. He did not walk off and let the wounded man make his own way, but the Samaritan carried him to a better place. Perhaps this illustrates that the body of Christ needs to carry the Holy Land. Israel during this regathering period is totally dependent on God's mercy, care and protection. His mercy is demonstrated on earth by those whom he has called and anointed for this purpose. In the parable, the man was in a weak condition and depended on others for life. Presently, Israel is being healed and restored by those who hear the call of God to bless His land and people.

4. He brought him to the inn and cared for him.

The Samaritan took upon himself the responsibility to see that the wounded man received all that he needed. He provided both rest and nourishment. Perhaps this illustrates the need for both the physical and spiritual aspects of strengthening. The body of Christ must likewise take the responsibility to see that Israel receives the fullness of care that will bring healing, strength and vitality. Renewed health and strength is a process and requires both time and commitment. A balanced commitment requires our material resources, as well as our time and personal effort. The quick fix arrangements so common in our society today will not solve the problem of long term responsibility.

It is plain from the parable that no one except the Samaritan took any responsibility. The responsibility rested solely on the Samaritan to provide God's mercy. The situation is the same today. If believers do not take the opportunity, who will?

5. He took care of him

The Samaritan continued to be concerned for the wounded man. He still was not able to provide for himself, so the Samaritan continued to provide for his care until he was restored. I believe this teaches us that believers must be prepared to stay with the task until it is completed. Not only are we required to be the good Samaritan with an immediate helping hand, but also to continue support. We may also need to enlist others to take part when needed. Total restoration is the goal. Believers have been blessed by God so they can provide for the nation of Israel and its people. God will continue to bless those who are committed to His pleasure.

Mercy: A Requirement

To demonstrate mercy is to demonstrate the likeness of Christ. As believers allow the living waters of "River Mercy" to flow through them, others also will feel and enjoy the refreshing waters of God's mercy. When people allow the waters of "River Merciless" to flow through them they demonstrate Satan's kingdom. Those who demonstrate mercy and those who demonstrate merciless life styles are worlds apart. (As far as heaven and hell).

The attributes of mercy take many forms and include: clemency, compassion, pity, tenderness, kindness, mildness, blessings, favor, pardon, graciousness, and forgiveness in all of its forms such as forgetting injuries, forgiving without being asked, and doing good in spite of ingratitude.

Those who are merciless also exhibit certain attributes. They are pitiless, cruel, unfeeling, unrelenting, severe, barbarous, unsparing, and lack compassion.

Mercy is important to God and should be just as important to us. The Bible says many things about mercy and puts a high priority on its attributes.

Mercy Defined

Mercy is sometimes defined as compassion. However, we can only understand real mercy in the context of God's love. We have no other basis for comprehending mercy. Therefore, genuine mercy to Israel can only be a reflection of God's mercy to us. Genuine mercy expressed through the power of Christ living within us is the only kind of mercy that will bring blessing to Israel, because it is the only kind that is truly genuine.

Genuine Mercy

The kind of mercy God expects from believers is revealed in the life of Jesus, Paul, the disciples, and the early church in Acts. It is a mercy that forgets about self and is singly focused on Christ and doing the pleasure of God. These lives all showed a common commitment to God's ways above personal ways and desires (Jesus, Php 2:5-11; Paul, Php 3:8; Disciples, Mt 19:27-30; Early church, Acts 4:32-37).

It is time that believers begin to express genuine mercy towards Israel. We need to give unconditionally, because we are servants, without expecting to receive blessings or rewards for doing good. Too much teaching today centers on doing God's pleasure for personal blessings and rewards. Being servants we should not expect rewards for being obedient, but God often gives them anyway.

Bible Instruction on Mercy

Believers are told to put on mercy (Col 3:12-13). This means to take on the fullness of its meaning and attributes. God also requires mercy from His people (Micah 6:8) and regards mercy greater than sacrifice (Mt 9:13, 12:7 & Hos 6:6). Without mercy all the good things we do will be of no benefit. Mercy is greater than the law. We are also told that to receive mercy from God, we must show mercy to others (Jas 2:13).

Power of Mercy

Mercy is very powerful. Through God's mercy, we have received salvation. As God's mercy flows through believers, others will also receive salvation including the House of Judah in the final days before Christ returns (Ro 11:31-32). Mercy multiplies and spreads as it flows from God through believers. Mercy has power over judgment (Jas 2:13) and purges iniquity (Pr 16:6). God's mercy has power to change people and change the world. Man has no power to change the world except through God's mercy.

Promises of Mercy

One of the greatest promises concerning mercy is that those who demonstrate mercy receive more (Mt 5:7). The Bible teaches that mercy comes from mercy. Seeds of mercy, once sown, will produce an abundant crop of the best kind of fruit. Mercy also brings the promise of favor with both God and man (Pr 3:3-4). Mercy brings goodness for the soul (Pr 11:17), happiness and life (Pr 14:21-22), righteousness and honor (Pr 21:21). Mercy is full of blessings to those who practice and develop its attributes.

Being Filled with Mercy

Being filled with mercy is being real, revealing the nature and image of God. Mercy brings the peace of God into lives and situations, and opens the door for God's love to flow out like a river of living water. It allows the fruit of the Holy Spirit to be manifested and appreciated. In many respects, mercy is the key that opens the doors to God's store house of blessings.

Being good stewards of God's mercy releases the unlimited rivers of the Holy Spirit. As believers allow that "river of mercy" to flow from them they will enjoy the spiritual vitality of a well watered garden (Isa 58).

10

DOING GOD'S PLEASURE

*"And they went forth, and preached everywhere,
the Lord working with them, and confirming the word,
with signs following."*
—Mark 16:20

Revelation from God requires a response from us (Eze 36:37). It also requires a commitment from which we can not draw back (Heb 10:38-39).

Mercy toward Israel by the Body of Christ will take many forms as the Holy Spirit directs the various giftings and ministries within the body. Some will pray and fast, some will go to Israel, some will tell the story, some will give money, and some may give their lives. The key is to get involved as did the Samaritan. Begin to make a difference and continue to release new life in Israel!

Every believer can be a partner in fulfilling God's plan for Israel by exhibiting a variety of practical attitudes and actions of friendship. As believers seek direction from God the Holy Spirit will lead each person in a path of fulfillment. Following are some examples of ways believers can be partners in blessing Israel.

Concern

Take an interest in Israel and relate to the things that pertain to the land and its people. Learn and read things about the land and keep current on events. Become involved in activities related to Israel. If possible visit Jerusalem and other parts of Israel. Besides receiving a personal blessing, visiting Israel is important for a number of reasons including the following:

1. It is the believer's capital city. It is the city of the great King, Jesus.
2. It gives honor to God. It acknowledges that Jerusalem is God's holy city.
3. It helps to bless and prosper the city.
4. It raises a standard against the enemies of Jerusalem.
5. It enables you to see the real Israel, not the one the news broadcast wants you to see. You can see first hand what God is doing!
6. Helps you pray for the City of Jerusalem.
7. Those who come and bless the city and pray for Jerusalem become a part of what God is doing in the land. The partnership is made stronger.

Intercession

"Pray for the peace of Jerusalem; they shall prosper that love thee. Peace be within thy walls, and prosperity within thy palaces. For my brethren and companions' sakes, I will now say, Peace be within thee. Because of the house of the Lord our God I will seek thy good."
—Psalm 122:6-9

Pray for the peace of Jerusalem and the Holy Land. God considers this important because believers are instructed to pray for Jerusalem (Ps 122: 6-9). When you pray for Jerusalem, you are praying for the whole earth because in God's view, Jerusalem is the world capital and blessings flow out of Jerusalem. When praying for Jerusalem, believers pray not only for the present day city to be blessed, but for the kingdom of God to come in its fullness and for the city to arise to its calling in Christ.

In reality, when believers pray according to Psalm 122, they pray for the return of Christ and His kingdom because only Jesus can fulfill that prayer for the city of Jerusalem. The Jerusalem that we are told to pray for is the Jerusalem that Paul calls the "mother of us all" (Gal 4:26), the Jerusalem Abraham looked for (Heb 11:10), and the Jerusalem we all wait for that is described in the late chapters of Revelation.

The peace of Jerusalem is God's ultimate goal on this earth, that His name be glorified. The world will never have peace until peace is established in Jerusalem. Only the Prince of Peace can bring real peace. The prayers of God's people are critical. Believers must remember to pray daily for Jerusalem. Prayers for Jerusalem will bless God and believers alike.

Honor

Give honor to Israel. Honor embodies many ideas such as esteem, dignity, reverence, celebration, nobleness, a good name, and respect. These all apply to believers attitudes and actions towards Israel. As we give honor to Israel we also give honor to God. The words of our mouth and our actions towards the house of Judah and the Holy Land need to reflect the fullness of these attitudes. Our thoughts, our words and our actions must all reflect God's view of the city and the land.

Gratitude

Express gratitude to Israel. God loves thankfulness. Every believer should be thankful to Israel and express a sense of obligation and good-will towards the land. Everything God has given us came through the Jewish people. This includes the Scriptures, Jesus and salvation. This attitude of gratitude towards Israel should be expressed openly to those around us.

Forgiveness

Walk in forgiveness. God requires an attitude of forgiveness in all situations from believers. If we want God's forgiveness, we must forgive others.

Love

Reflect an attitude of love towards Israel. Jesus said, *"he that hath seen me hath seen the father"* (Jn 14:9), He also said, *"if you love me keep my commandments" (Jn 14:15)*. As we have the mind of Christ our desires will conform to God's desires. As a result, our primary goal will be to please the Father and become one with Him. We can not love the Father without loving Jesus, nor can we love Jesus (who was born a Jew) without loving the house of Judah. Our attitude towards Israel will reflect our attitude towards God! The two are yoked together!

Giving

Give generously. A giving and a generous attitude brings God's blessings. As we sow seeds of blessings, we will receive the fruit of blessings. As we bless Israel by giving of our time, energies, and material support, God will give abundant blessings back. But even if we receive nothing in return, we are still obligated to bless Israel out of debt and obedience. We should want to bless Israel just for the opportunity to bless God, without reward.

Friendship

Be an active friend of Israel. It is very important that believers be friends of Israel. Trusted and true friendship is critical. Being friends can take many different forms. For some it may mean a close intimate relationship with the nation or individual people. For others it may be more of an encourager, well-wisher, advocate, defender or neighbor type of relationship. These are all attitudes and actions that are pleasing to God. All believers can exhibit some type of friendship with Israel.

Serving

Find opportunities to serve Israel. Jesus came to earth as a humble servant and said that those who follow Him should have a servants attitude. Serving involves more than waiting on someone. It also involves helping, assisting, ministering, and fulfilling ones duty. Serving means putting others ahead of self.

Peacemakers

Be a peacemaker. God has high regard for peacemakers. On the other hand He judges those who cause trouble and strife. Peacemakers include intercessors, as well as mediators, arbitrators, and pacifists.

Peace is God's desire for Jerusalem and the Holy Land. The Church of Jesus Christ must play a major role in bringing peace to the land because true peace can come only from the Prince of Peace, Jesus. Only the church has the gospel of peace. The world has no ability to bring peace, only those under the power of the Holy Spirit have the ability to bring peace to men or nations. The land and the people are now calling out for peace and God has pushed the doors wide open for His peacemakers to get involved. Now is the time!

Mercy

Show God's mercy to Israel. For believers, mercy is the key to blessing Israel in these last days. Believers have experienced God's great mercy and therefore must allow that mercy to flow into Israel. Anyone exhibiting genuine mercy can not help but have a positive influence on Israel. God's mercy embodies both God's love and the fruit of the Holy Spirit. Seek to manifest the fruit of God's mercy.

Kindness

Extend kindness to Israel. Being humane, friendly, good-natured, charitable and sympathetic all involve kindness. As we extend kindness to Israel God will also treat us with kindness.

Freedom

Proclaim liberty to the captives. We have been set free through Jesus. We also should make every effort to set the house of Judah free in Christ from every bondage and oppression.

Strengthen

Use every means to strengthen the land. Many would try to weaken and spoil Israel in Satan's name. However, believers in Jesus have the responsibility to raise a standard against the enemies of Israel in the name of Jesus. Believers should use every means to strengthen the land of Israel. We have mighty weapons in the spiritual realm for the bringing down of strongholds (2 Cor 10:4-5).

Build

Begin to build in Israel. Many would try to break down and destroy, but believers need to be about the task of building. Building includes both material and spiritual aspects. In the name of Jesus, believers can overcome evil with good and build and strengthen the nation of Israel. One thing is clear in Scriptures, as we give out mercy to do God's pleasure, more abundant mercy will be given to us.

Israel will be the glory of the whole earth. The resources of all heaven and earth are available to those who bless Israel in these days. As believers rebuild the city and lay the foundation of the temple, they will be a channel for the resources of this world to flow into Israel. Eventually all the world's resources will flow into Israel *"because the abundance of the sea shall be converted unto thee, and the forces of the Gentiles shall come unto thee"* (Isa 60:5). The gates of Jerusalem shall be open continually, *"that men may bring unto thee the forces of the Gentiles"* (Isa 60:11).

Currently, the world's wealth and the gospel are spread throughout the gentile nations, but all things belong to God and He will return the earth's wealth unto Jerusalem as Jesus sets up His throne in the Holy City.

As the early church was of one heart and soul and gave what they had, there was no lack (Ac 4:32-35). Such too will be the case as believers give to Israel in unity.

More is required than the usual stock answers, sermons, tracts and the like. Be a friend and become an instrument of God's love and mercy. Mercy is the answer, not programs and methods that promote man's ways. Man's traditional methods will only bring a remnant to Jesus. As the Spirit of God removes the veil and engraves the hearts of His people with His word, a mighty outpouring of the latter day rains will bring the house of Judah to Christ our King.

Mercy and love demonstrated through the power of the Holy Spirit alone has the power to release the heavenly anointing to go forth and stir up the spirit of God's people throughout the Holy Land.

Involvement

Get involved with groups in Israel. Many, many activities are taking place in Israel. Numerous individuals and organizations are involved in a wide diversity of projects. Many of these projects welcome participation in various ways. In some, you can participate without leaving your home, while others require travel to Israel.

Like any ministries, some are pure before God and others are done in self-interest. Also, men and ministries change with time. I would not judge, comment or make any specific suggestions regarding any work in Israel. Only God knows the hearts of men and what is right for you. Allow the Holy Spirit to direct you to those ministries or groups that are right for you. Seek God!

The important thing is for each person to become involved with God's plan for Israel in the way He wants you to be involved. God has given you many gifts and talents designed specifically for you to benefit His kingdom.

Also, you can do many things on your own without the association of a ministry or organization. God does not need men's organizations to accomplish His work, He needs only obedient servants that listen to the Holy Spirit.

11

CONCLUSION

*"The wilderness and the solitary place shall be glad for them;
and the desert shall rejoice, and blossom as the rose.
It shall blossom abundantly, and rejoice even with joy and singing:
the glory of Lebanon shall be given unto it,
the excellency of Carmel and Sharon,
they shall see the glory of the Lord,
and the excellency of our God."*
—Isaiah 35:1-2

Is this the generation that all history has been waiting for and God's prophets have talked about for thousands of years? If so, in this current generation God is bringing all history into focus as he unites heaven and earth. God is preparing the earth for the return of His Son, Jesus Christ. If this is that time then the body of believers on the earth today are in a unique situation to be used of God to help bring about His ultimate pleasure in the restoration of His nation and people that His name will be glorified in both heaven and earth.

Believers alive in this last segment of time as we know it can not pass up the glorious opportunity to be partners in God's work. It is time for believers to get involved in one of the greatest events of history and help proclaim the glorious way of the Lord.

Get involved in blessing the Holy Land of Israel and its people as the Lord directs. There is much to do and the time is now. Today is the time to build the city and lay the foundation of the temple that God's glory will fill the earth. Now is the time to call forth Jerusalem to arise and be adorned for her King.

Recent trips to Israel have confirmed what the Lord is doing in the Holy Land and allowed me to see and experience first hand the marvelous works of God throughout His favorite place on earth. Truly the Lord is working a work in the land, like in the days of Habakkuk (1:5), that is so great, that even if told, men would not believe.

The daily news broadcasts constantly try to obscure God's working in the land by reporting all the negative aspects of what is taking place in Israel (Satan's activities in the land). That is only a small part of what is taking place in the Holy Land (far out of proportion). The land is being blessed abundantly and many more good things are taking place each day than bad. The Spirit of the Living God is manifesting the glory of God daily in new and fresh ways.

Sovereign, momentous moves of God are common throughout the land on a regular basis, which no man or ministry can claim credit, because God is going to bring glory to His name. The kingdom of heaven is increasingly being manifested throughout Jerusalem and the Holy Land.

Regions and towns that have been completely closed to the Gospel of Jesus Christ for many many years are now open and in some places welcome it. As a result, villages and towns throughout Israel have a true Christian segment.

Signs and wonders are being observed throughout the cities and the land. Extraordinary events involving heavenly messengers are being experienced increasingly. Believers are being called to Jerusalem from throughout the earth to carry out God's instructions. God's people are being sent from Jerusalem to the ends of the earth with the Gospel message. The land, the cities and the people are responding to the prophetic words of God's holy prophets.

Is it any wonder that Satan continues to stir up trouble in the region? He knows the time is short and the tide of battle is turning against him as the armies of God are sent forth to complete the land for the return of Jesus.

Other important events are also taking place in Jerusalem. Consider the following examples: growth of Jewish believers throughout Israel and in Jerusalem (the percentage is still small but growth is rapid), rapid development of the city into a major international center with people from all nations, and prosperity throughout the region.

A marvelous event is occurring across the Holy Land. Is it possible that God is removing the covering from over the land as He has promised to do? *"And he will destroy in this mountain the face of the covering cast over all people, and the veil that is spread over all nations"* Isaiah 25:7. Will this be followed by the return of the cherubim with the glory of the Lord to rest on Jerusalem (Eze 43:1-5) in like manner that it went (Eze 11:22-25)? God has said that the cherubim will return with His glory to the land.

While much has taken place in recent years, I believe we are just starting to witness what God has planned for the Holy Land. The pace of events is accelerating. We stand on the threshold of great and marvelous things as God's glory is being revealed in new ways. The earth will see the power and glory of God in ways that no past generation has observed as Jesus prepares His land and people for His return to earth. Rejoice, be a part of what God is doing in Israel and be blessed in the process.

"Pray for the peace of Jerusalem: they shall prosper that love thee. Peace be within thy walls, and prosperity within thy palaces. For my brethren and companions' sakes, I will now say Peace be within thee. Because of the house of the Lord I will seek thy good."
Psalm 122:6-9

"Rejoice ye with Jerusalem, and be glad with her, all ye that love her: rejoice for joy with her, all ye that mourn for her: That ye may suck, and be satisfied with the breasts of her consolations; that ye may milk out, and be delighted with the abundance of her glory. For thus saith the LORD,

Behold, I will extend peace to her like a river, and the glory of the Gentiles like a flowing stream: then shall ye suck, ye shall be borne upon her sides, and be dandled upon her knees. As one whom his mother comforteth, so will I comfort you; and ye shall be comforted in Jerusalem. And when ye see this, your heart shall rejoice, and your bones shall flourish like an herb: and the hand of the LORD shall be known toward his servants, and his indignation toward his enemies.

Isaiah 66:10-14

A Garden of Eden

Arise, O city of gardens, most beautiful.
Men shall liken you to the garden of Eden.
Every good and pleasant tree shall cover thee.

The Lord God Almighty hath planted His garden.
He hath filled thee with tilled cities.
Thy land shall overflow with harvest.

You will be watered by the rivers of life.
Your trees of life will established deep roots.
Your people and flocks shall prosper.

Let your desolate places become gardens.
Let your ruined cities become fenced.
Let your flock prosper in health and peace.

The Lord of hosts shall again walk in your gardens.
Joy and peace shall spring forth from within.
A garden like the garden of Eden will flourish.